NEW MEXICO PHARMAC

MW00934316

MPJE COMPREHENSIVE REVIEW

Joshua Scott, PharmD

Second Edition

Table of Contents   **Pages**

PART ONE

PART TWO

PART ONE

NEW MEXICO PHARMACY LAW

- The objective this regulation is to establish the location for regular meetings of the board, designate persons to preside overboard meetings, establish standards for employees and members who are required to give surety bonds, and provide for employee job descriptions and a registry of pharmacists.

- The chairman of the board shall preside at all meetings, preserve order, appoint committees, and decide all questions of order subject to appeal to the board. In the absence of the chairman, the vice-chairman or a member of the board shall preside.

- Meetings shall be held in the office of the board unless a waiver is requested by most of the board.

- Examinations shall be administered at a place or location specified by the board.

- The duties and responsibilities of the executive director or any employee of this board shall be those which are detailed in the job descriptions filed with the state personnel department.

- Registry of pharmacists to be maintained by the board shall record the name, registry number, date of registration, grades of examination by subject, and if by reciprocity, the name of the state from which examined.

- All written and oral communication made by any person to the board or any committee of the board relating to actual or potential disciplinary action, which includes complaints made to the board or the committee, shall be confidential communications and are not public records for the purposes of the Inspection of Public Records Act.

- All data, communications and information acquired, prepared or disseminated by the board or a committee relating to actual or potential disciplinary action or its investigation of complaints shall not be disclosed except to the extent necessary to carry out the purposes of the board or the committee or in a judicial appeal from the actions of the board or the committee or in a referral of cases made to law enforcement agencies, national database clearinghouses or other licensing boards.

- Information contained in complaint files is public information and subject to disclosure when the board or the committee acts on a complaint and issues a notice of contemplated action or reaches a settlement prior to the issuance of a notice of contemplated action.

16.19.4.10

CONTINUING PHARMACY EDUCATION REQUIREMENTS:

- Continuing pharmacy education certified as completed by an approved provider will be required of a registered pharmacist who applies for renewal of New Mexico registration as follows: 3.0 CEU (30 contact hours) every two years. Effective January 1, 2013, pharmacist and pharmacist clinician renewal applications shall document.

16.19.4.11

CONSULTANT PHARMACIST:

Duties and responsibilities:

- To abide by the code of ethics of the American society of consultant pharmacists. Must be qualified to practice as a consultant pharmacist and is to be aware of all federal and state drug laws, rules and regulations related to pharmacy services, and to provide the facility with current information pertaining to drug service.

- Ensure that drugs are handled in the facility in which he/she is the consultant pharmacist, in a manner that protect the safety and welfare of the patient.

- Set the policy and procedures in the facility as related to all facits of drug handling and distribution; these policies and procedures to be reviewed and updated on an annual basis.

- To visit the facility, commensurate with his duties, as specified by board regulations relative to the facility or by written contract with the administration of the facility not inconsistent with board regulations.

- His/her primary goal and objective shall be the health and safety of the patient, and he/she shall make every effort to assure the maximum level of safety and efficacy in the provision of pharmaceutical services.

- The consultant pharmacist shall not condone or participate in any transaction with any practitioner of another health profession, or any other persons whosoever under which fees are divided, or rebates or kickbacks paid or caused to be paid, or which may result in financial exploitation of patients or their families in connection with the provision of drugs and medication or supplies or pharmaceutical services.

- Consultant pharmacist serving skilled nursing facilities and intermediate care facilities - upper-level care - long term care facilities by any other title:

- The consultant pharmacist's agreement with the facility shall include but is not limited to the following duties and responsibilities.

- Serve as a member of appropriate committees and attend these meetings.

- Development of the drug control procedures manual.

- Monitor on a routine basis all aspects of the total drug distribution system - to be accomplished in a manner designed to monitor and safeguard all areas of the drug distribution system.

- Maintain active pharmacist status registration in the state.

- Assume responsibility for the destruction or removal of unwanted dangerous drugs and any controlled substances as prescribed by law and regulations.

- Maintain a log of all visits and activities in the facility indicating dates and other pertinent data; such logs are to be available to inspection by state drug inspectors upon request.

- Furnish and replenish emergency drug supply in acceptable containers. Maintain a log of use and replacement of drugs in the emergency tray.

- Make routine inspections of drug storage areas, patient health records, and review drug regimen of each patient at least once a month. Report irregularities, contraindication, drug interactions, etc., to the medical staff.

- Provide or make arrangements for provision of pharmacy services to the facility on a 24-hour, seven days a week basis, including stat orders.

- Provide in-service training of staff personnel as outlined in the procedure's manual.

- Meet all other responsibilities of a consultant pharmacist as set forth in the board regulations and federal or state laws and which are consistent with quality patient care.

16.19.4.13

CHANGE OF ADDRESS:

- Any registrant or licensee shall report in writing any change of address or employment to the board within 10 days.

16.19.4.14

ACTIVE STATUS:

- Any pharmacist who maintains competency through the development and maintenance of knowledge, skill and aptitude, to ensure continuing competence as a pharmacy professional, and is able to demonstrate to the board said competence in the practice of pharmacy shall be issued an active license. Records of continuing education or continuous professional development shall be maintained and available for inspection by the board or the board's agent. A pharmacist shall be issued an active status license upon proper application and payment of fees.

16.19.4.15

INACTIVE STATUS:

- A pharmacist not engaged or ceasing to be engaged in the practice of pharmacy for more than one year shall be issued an inactive status license upon proper application and payment of fees.
- Pursuant to Section 61-11-13. B, an inactive status pharmacist applying for an active status license, who has not been actively engaged in pharmacy for over one year, may be required to serve an internship training program and submit evidence of continuing education relating to the practice of pharmacy, as required by Section 61-11-6 and Section 61-11-13 and the board regulations.

16.19.4.16

RESPONSIBILITIES OF PHARMACIST AND PHARMACIST INTERN:

- The following responsibilities require the use of professional judgement and therefore shall be performed only by a pharmacist or pharmacist intern:
    - receipt of all new verbal prescription orders and reduction to writing.
    - initial identification, evaluation and interpretation of the prescription order and any necessary clinical clarification prior to dispensing.
    - professional consultation with a patient or his agent regarding a prescription.
    - evaluation of available clinical data in patient medication record system.
    - oral communication with the patient or patient's agent of information, as defined in this section under patient counseling, in order to improve therapy by ensuring proper use of drugs and devices.
    - professional consultation with the prescriber, the prescriber's agent, or any other health care professional or authorized agent regarding a patient and any medical information pertaining to the prescription.
    - drug regimen review, as defined in 61-11-2L.
    - professional consultation, without dispensing, will require that the patient be provided with the identification of the pharmacist or pharmacy intern providing the service.
- Only a pharmacist shall perform the following duties:
    - final check on all aspects of the completed prescription including sterile products and cytotoxic preparations, and assumption of the responsibility for the filled

prescription, including, but not limited to, appropriateness of dose, accuracy of drug, strength, labeling, verification of ingredients and proper container.

- o evaluation of pharmaceuticals for formulary selection within the facility.
- o supervision of all supportive personnel activities including preparation, mixing, assembling, packaging, labeling and storage of medications.
- o ensure that supportive personnel have been properly trained for the duties they may perform;
- o any verbal communication with a patient or patient's representative regarding a change in drug therapy or performing therapeutic interchanges (i.e., drugs with similar effects in specific therapeutic categories); this does not apply to substitution of generic equivalents.
- o any other duty required of a pharmacist by any federal or state law.

- Patient records.
- A reasonable effort must be made to obtain, record, and maintain at least the following information:
  - o name, address, telephone number, date of birth (or age) and gender of the patient.
  - o individual medical history, if significant, including disease state or states, known allergies and drug reactions and a comprehensive list of medications and relevant devices; and
  - o pharmacists comment relevant to the individual's drug therapy.
- Such information contained in the patient record should be considered by the pharmacist or pharmacist intern in the exercise of their professional judgement concerning both the offer to counsel and the content of counseling.
- Prospective drug review.

- Prior to dispensing any prescription, a pharmacist shall review the patient profile for the purpose of identifying:
  - clinical abuse/misuse.
  - therapeutic duplication.
  - drug-disease contraindications.
  - drug-drug interactions.
  - incorrect drug dosage.
  - incorrect duration of drug treatment.
  - drug-allergy interactions.
  - appropriate medication indication.

16.19.6.9

PHARMACIST-IN-CHARGE:

- The term "pharmacist-in-charge" means a pharmacist licensee in the state of New Mexico who has been designated pharmacist-in-charge pursuant to Section 61-11-15 NMSA 1978. Failure to perform any of the following duties will constitute a violation of Paragraph (1) of Subsection A of Section 61-11-20 NMSA 1978. It shall be the duty and responsibility of the pharmacist-in-charge consistent with the regulations governing professional conduct and in compliance with all applicable laws and regulations:
  - to establish for the employees of the pharmacy, written policies and procedures for procurement, storage, compounding and dispensing of drugs:
  - the procurement, storage, compounding and dispensing of drugs.

- o the operation and security for remote pharmacist drug utilization review sites where applicable.

- o error prevention and reporting procedures according to the requirements of 16.19.25.8 NMAC.

- o to supervise all of the professional employees of the pharmacy.

- o to supervise all of the non-professional employees of the pharmacy in so far as their duties relate to the sale and storage of drugs.

- o to establish and supervise the method and manner for the storing and safekeeping of drugs.

- o to establish and supervise the record keeping system for the purchase, sale, possession, storage, safekeeping and return of drugs.

- o to notify the board immediately upon his knowledge that his service as pharmacist-in-charge have been or will be terminated.

- o inform the board in writing, within 10 days of the employment or termination of any pharmacy technician; the information shall include name and location of pharmacy, name of employee, social security number, and date of hire or termination.

- o to complete the New Mexico board of pharmacy self-assessment inspection form as provided by the board and to submit the signed and dated form with the pharmacy renewal application to the board office.

- Every licensed pharmacy will be under continued daily supervision of a registered pharmacist who shall have direct control of the pharmaceutical affairs of the pharmacy.

- Upon termination of the pharmacist-in-charge each pharmacy owner shall immediately designate a successor pharmacist-in-charge and immediately notify the state board of pharmacy of such designation. The owner shall request the license application form to be completed by the successor pharmacist-in-charge and filed with the board within 10 days. The failure to designate a successor pharmacist-in-charge and notify the board of such designation shall be deemed a violation of the Pharmacy Act, Section 61-11-15 NMSA 1978.

16.19.6.10

MINIMUM STANDARDS:

- The restricted area to be occupied by the prescription department shall be an undivided area of not less than 240 square feet. The floor area shall extend the full length of the prescription compounding counter. This area shall provide for the compounding and dispensing and storage of all dangerous or restricted drugs, pharmaceuticals, or chemicals under proper condition of sanitation, temperature, light, ventilation, segregation and security. No space in this area shall provide for an office, auxiliary storeroom or public restroom(s).

- A private restroom, for exclusive use by the pharmacy staff, may be attached to the restricted area. This restroom does not count as square footage for the restricted area.

- An office for the exclusive use by the pharmacy may be attached to the restricted area. No general store accounting functions may be performed in this office. This area will not be considered as square footage for the restricted area.

- An auxiliary storage area for the exclusive use of the pharmacy may be attached to the restricted area. No items may be stored in this area that are not directly related to the operations performed in the restricted area. This area will not be considered as square footage for the restricted area.

- Each pharmacy shall provide facilities whereby a pharmacist may professionally counsel a patient or a patients' agent and protect the right to privacy and confidentiality.

- An exception to the minimum space footage requirement may be considered by the board on an individual basis. The board may consider such factors as:

- Rural area location with small population.

- No pharmacy within the same geographical area.

- No prescription area of less than 120 square feet will be acceptable.

- All special waivers will be subject to review annually for reconsideration.

- The prescription compounding counter must provide a minimum of 16 square feet of unobstructed compounding and dispensing space for one pharmacist and a minimum of 24 square feet for two or more pharmacists when on duty concurrently. The counter shall be of adequate height of at least 36 inches, if necessary, five percent or at least one workstation will comply with the American with Disabilities Act.

- The restricted floor area shall be unobstructed for a minimum width of 30 inches from the prescription compounding center.

- The pharmacy restricted area shall be separated from the merchandising area by a barrier of sufficient height and depth to render the dangerous drugs within the pharmacy inaccessible to the reach of any unauthorized person. All windows, doors, and gates to the restricted area shall be equipped with secure locks. The restricted area shall be locked in the absence of a pharmacist on the premises.

- The restricted area shall contain an adequate sink with hot and cold water.

- The restricted area shall contain a refrigerator capable of maintaining the adequate temperature

- The restricted area of a retail pharmacy established in conjunction with any other business other than a retail drug store, shall be separated from the merchandising area of the other business by a permanent barrier or partition from floor to roof with entry doors that may be securely locked when a pharmacist is not on duty.

16.19.6.11

MINIMUM EQUIPMENT AND ACCESSORY STANDARDS:

- The pharmacy shall have the necessary equipment for the safe and appropriate storage, compounding, packaging, labeling, dispensing and preparations of drugs and parenteral products appropriate to the scope of pharmaceutical services provided. The following items shall be in the pharmacy; an updated reference source, appropriate to each practice site, either electronic or paper version; and one copy of the most recently published New Mexico pharmacy laws, rules and regulations and available revisions, either electronic or paper version.

16.19.6.12

NOTICE OF EMPLOYEE CHANGE:

- Proprietors of pharmacies must report on the annual application for renewal of pharmacy license the names and registry numbers of all registered pharmacist employees and registered interns and shall notify the secretary of the board of pharmacy within 10 days, in writing, of any change in personnel.

16.19.6.14

PROHIBITION OF RESALE OF DRUGS:

- Drugs, medicines, sickroom supplies and items of personal hygiene shall not be accepted for return or exchange of any pharmacist or pharmacy after such articles have been taken from the premises where sold or distributed.

- Prescriptions returned to stock: The pharmacy shall maintain a record of prescriptions which are returned to stock. The record shall include patient name, date filled, prescription number, drug name, drug strength, and drug quantity. The record shall be retrievable within 72 hours.

16.19.6.15

DISPOSITION OF DANGEROUS DRUGS OR CONTROLLED SUBSTANCES:

- Permission shall be obtained, in writing, from the board, after inspection, before any inventory of dangerous drugs or controlled substances may be sold, transferred, disposed of, or otherwise removed from the current premises. All sales shall be subject to the laws of the state.

- Dispensed pharmaceuticals, collection, and disposal: Patient dispensed legend and OTC medications that are unwanted or expired may be returned to an authorized pharmacy for destruction. The pharmacy must submit a protocol or subsequent changes to the board or the board's agent, for approval. Once approved the pharmacy is authorized to collect pharmaceuticals for destruction. A protocol is to be submitted to the board of pharmacy for staff approval. Such protocol must include:

- Secure and enclosed collection unit that does not allow for unauthorized access.

- A description of the dedicated area for collection unit inside the pharmacy within site of the authorized pharmacy staff.

- Direction of collection that allows for safe and secure disposition.

- Name of contracted disposal company that is licensed for pharmaceutical destruction.

- Frequency of collection and destruction by the disposal company.

- Records of collection and destruction supplied by the disposal company.

- Items accepted at a take back site may include:
  - dangerous drugs (prescription drugs).
  - controlled substances if authorized under federal law or rule.
  - over the counter medications.
  - veterinary medications.
  - medicated ointments and lotions.
  - liquid medication in glass or leak-proof containers.

- Items NOT accepted at a take back site may include:
  - needles.
  - thermometers.
  - bloody or infectious waste.
  - personal care products.
  - controlled substances (unless authorized by federal law).
  - hydrogen peroxide.

- o empty containers.

- o business waste.

- Collected medications are not for re-dispensing.

- Directions for take back for patients and list of accepted and non-accepted products must be posted on the collection unit.

- Suspension of the pharmacy's authority to collect and dispose of dispensed pharmaceutical shall occur upon violation of the approved protocol. The pharmacy may petition the board for removal of that suspension.

16.19.6.16

ROBBERY, BURGLARY, FIRE, FLOOD REPORT:

- When a pharmacy is involved in a robbery, burglary, fire, flood, or any unusual event in which dangerous drugs might be missing or damaged, the owner shall immediately file with the board a signed statement of the circumstances of such occurrence and evidence that local authorities were notified, if applicable.

- When a business is sold or an ownership transfer is initiated and a new license application is submitted, the board may require examination of any stock which may be determined to be adulterated, deteriorated or questionable quality. Merchandise considered to be unfitted for sale may be embargoed if the owner does not voluntarily consent to destruction. In the event the drugs are embargoed, the owner of the product must bear the expense of assay to prove purity, strength, and product quality.

16.19.6.19

CHANGE IN LOCATION OF A PHARMACY:

- Before a licensed pharmacy changes the location of the business, or the physical dimensions or elements of physical security, a new application shall be submitted to the board, setting forth such changes. Upon approval and completion of the change, a request for inspection will be submitted to the chief inspector. There will be no charge for the new application, but the inspection will carry the same fee as applies for a new pharmacy inspection.

16.19.6.20

TRANSFER OF OWNERSHIP:

- A transfer of ownership occurs upon.

- The sale of the pharmacy to another individual or individuals by the present owner.

- The addition or deletion of one or more partners in a partnership.

- The death of a singular or sole owner.

- The change of ownership of thirty percent or more of the voting stock of a corporation since the issuance of the license or last renewal application. A new license application will be required to be filed in each of the above circumstances. As stated in the Pharmacy Act, Subsection I of Section 61-11-14 NMSA 1978, licenses are not transferable, and shall expire on December 31 of each year unless renewed.

16.19.6.22

COMPUTERIZED PRESCRIPTION INFORMATION:

- Computers for the storage and retrieval of prescription information do not replace the requirement that a prescription written by a practitioner or telephoned to the pharmacist by a practitioner and reduced to hardcopy be retained as permanent record. Computers shall be maintained as required by the Pharmacy Act; the Drug, Device, and Cosmetic Act; the Controlled Substance Act; and the board of pharmacy regulations.

- The computer shall be capable of producing a printout of prescription information within a 72-hour period on demand, with certification by the practitioner stating it is a true and accurate record. Requested printouts include patient specific; practitioner specific; drug specific; or date specific reports. The printout shall include:
  - o   the original prescription numbers.
  - o   the practitioner's name
  - o   full name and address of patient.
  - o   date of issuance of original prescription order by the practitioner and the date filled.
  - o   name, strength, dosage form, quantity of drug prescribed.
  - o   total number of refills authorized by the practitioner.
  - o   the quantity dispensed is different than the quantity prescribed, then record of the quantity dispensed.
  - o   in the case of a controlled substance, the name, address and DEA registration number of the practitioner and the schedule of the drug.
  - o   identification of the dispensing pharmacist; computer-generated pharmacist initials are considered to be the pharmacist of record unless overridden manually by a

20

different pharmacist who will be the pharmacist of record.

- Permanent records of electronic prescriptions, transmitted directly over approved secure electronic prescribing networks or other board approved transmissions standards, do not have to be reduced to hardcopy provided the following requirements are met.

- Electronic prescription information or data must be maintained in the original format received for 10 years.

- Documentation of business associate agreements with "network vendors", electronic prescription transmission intermediaries and pharmacy software vendors involved in the transmission and formatting of the prescription who can provide documentation of chain of trust of who has had access to prescription content is available.

- Reliable backup copies of the information are available and stored in a secure manner as approved by the board.

- All elements required on a prescription and record keeping requirements are fulfilled including identification of the dispensing pharmacist of record.

- Electronically archived prescription records of scanned images of indirect written or faxed prescriptions are permitted provided the following requirements are met:
  - images of scanned prescriptions are readily retrievable and can be reproduces in a manner consistent with state and federal laws within a 72-hour period.
  - the identity of the pharmacist approving the scanned imaging and of the pharmacist responsible for destroying the original document after three years is clearly documented.
  - the electronic form shows the exact and legible image of the original prescription.
  - the original paper prescription document must be maintained for a minimum of

- three years and the electronic image of the prescription for 10 years.

- the prescription is not for a controlled substance except as allowed by federal law.

- reliable backup copies of the information are available and stored in a secure manner as approved by the board.

- all elements required on a prescription and record keeping requirements are fulfilled including identification of the dispensing pharmacist of record.

- the original paper prescription document for a non-controlled substance must be maintained on the licensed premises for a period of 120 days from the initial date of dispensing.

- the original paper prescription document for a controlled substance must be maintained on the licensed premises for a period of two years from the initial date of dispensing.

- Electronic records of prescriptions and patient prescription records may be stored offsite on secure electronic servers provided the following requirements are met:

  - records are readily retrievable.

  - all Health Insurance Portability and Accountability Act and board of pharmacy patient privacy requirements are met.

  - reliable backup copies of the information are available and stored in a secure manner as approved by the board.

- Original paper prescription documents may be stored offsite after the minimum period of storage on the licensed premises has been reached, provided that the following requirements are met:

- the storage area is maintained so that records are secure and prevented from unauthorized access.

- the storage area is maintained with appropriate fire suppression safeguards and climate control capabilities.

- all Health Insurance Portability and Accountability Act and board of pharmacy patient privacy requirements are met.

- the pharmacist-in charge maintains a record-keeping system that records storage location(s) and documents an inventory of original paper prescription documents that are maintained offsite.

- original paper prescription records must be able to be produced within three business days upon the request of the board or an authorized officer of the law.

16.19.6.23

PRESCRIPTIONS:

- A valid prescription is an order for a dangerous drug given individually for the person for whom prescribed, either directly from the prescribing practitioner to the pharmacist, or indirectly by means of a written order signed by the practitioner.

- A prescription may be prepared by a secretary or agent, i.e., office nurse under supervision, for the signature of the practitioner and where applicable; a prescription may be communicated to the pharmacist by an employee or agent of the registered practitioner. The prescribing practitioner is responsible in case the prescription does not conform in all essential respects to the law and regulation.

- Prescription information received from a patient, other than a signed written prescription from a practitioner, has no legal status as a valid prescription. A pharmacist receiving such prescription information must contact the prescribing physician for a new prescription.

- Exchange of prescription information between pharmacies for the purpose of filling or refilling is authorized under the following conditions only.

- The original prescription entry shall be marked in the pharmacy computer system. Pharmacies not using a computer shall mark the hard copy.

- The prescription shall indicate that it has been transferred and pharmacy location and file number of the original prescription.

- In addition to all information required to appear on a prescription, the prescription shall show the date of original fillings as well as the number of valid refills remaining.

- An original unfilled non-controlled substance prescription that is transferred shall be subject to the same record keeping requirements as filled prescriptions.

- Transfer or forwarding of controlled substance prescriptions shall not be allowed electronically except as permitted by federal law. Any transfer of controlled substances listed in Schedules III, IV, and V must be within any rule adopted by the federal DEA under Title 21 CFR 1306.25, for refill purposes.

- A pharmacy may not refuse to transfer original prescription information to another pharmacy who is acting on behalf of a patient and who is making a request for this information as specified in this subsection. The transfer of original prescription information must be done in a timely manner.

- Fax Machines: Fax prescription means a valid prescription which is transmitted by an electronic device which sends an exact image of a written prescription signed by the practitioner to a pharmacy. The prescribing of controlled substances by fax must comply with all state and federal laws. No pharmacist may dispense a drug solely on the basis of a prescription received by fax except under the following circumstances:

- o the pharmacist shall exercise professional judgment regarding the accuracy and authenticity of the prescription consistent with existing federal and state statutes and regulations.

- o the original fax prescription shall be printed and stored in the pharmacy as required by state and federal law and board rules and may serve as the record of the prescription.

- o the fax prescription shall include name and fax number of the pharmacy, the prescriber's phone number, for verbal confirmation, time and date of transmission, as well as any other information required by federal and state statute or regulation.

- o in institutional practice, the fax machine operator must be identified by a statement in the facility policy and procedures manual.

- o the receiving fax machine must be physically located in a restricted area to protect patient confidentiality.

16.19.6.25

CENTRALIZED PRESCRIPTION DISPENSING:

- A retail pharmacy may outsource prescription drug order dispensing to another retail or nonresident pharmacy provided the pharmacies:
  - o have the same owner or.

- have entered into a written contract or agreement which outlines the services to be provided and the responsibilities and accountabilities of each pharmacy in compliance with federal and state laws and regulations; and
- share a common electronic file or have appropriate technology to allow access to sufficient information necessary or required to dispense or process a prescription drug order.

- The pharmacist-in-charge of the dispensing pharmacy shall ensure that:
  - the pharmacy maintains and uses adequate storage or shipment containers and shipping processes to ensure drug stability and potency; such shipping processes shall include the use of appropriate packaging material or devices to ensure that the drug is maintained at an appropriate temperature range to maintain the integrity of the medication throughout the delivery process; and
  - the dispensed prescriptions are shipped in containers which are sealed in a manner as to show evidence of opening or tampering.
  - A retail or nonresidential dispensing pharmacy shall comply with the provisions of 16.19.6 NMAC and this section.

Notifications to patients.

- A pharmacy that out-sources prescription dispensing to another pharmacy shall prior to outsourcing the prescription:
  - notify patients that their prescription may be outsourced to another pharmacy; and
  - give the name of that pharmacy or if the pharmacy is part of a network of pharmacies under common ownership and any of the network of pharmacies may dispense the prescription, the patient shall be notified of this fact; such notification

may be provided through a one-time written notice to the patient or through the use of a sign in the pharmacy; and

- If the prescription is delivered directly to the patient by the dispensing pharmacy upon request by the patient and not returned to the requesting pharmacy, the pharmacist employed by the dispensing pharmacy shall ensure that the patient receives written notice of available counseling; such notice shall include days and hours of availability and his or her right to request counseling and a toll-free number from which the patient or patient's agent may obtain oral counseling from a pharmacist who has ready access to the patient's record; for pharmacies delivering more than fifty percent of their prescriptions by mail or other common carrier, the hours of availability shall be a minimum of 60 hours per week and not less than six days per week; the facility must have sufficient toll-free phone lines and personnel to provide counseling within 15 minutes.

Prescription labeling.

- The dispensing pharmacy shall place on the prescription label the name and address or name and pharmacy license number of the pharmacy dispensing the prescription and the name and address of the pharmacy which receives the dispensed prescription.

- The dispensing pharmacy shall indicate in some manner which pharmacy dispensed the prescription (e.g., filled by ABC pharmacy for XYZ pharmacy) and comply with all other prescription labeling requirements.

Policies and Procedures.

- A policy and procedure manual as it relates to centralized dispensing shall be maintained at both pharmacies and be approved by the board or its' agent and be available for inspection.

27

Each pharmacy is required to maintain only those portions of the policy and procedure manual that relate to that pharmacy's operations. The manual shall:

- o outline the responsibilities of each of the pharmacies.
- o include a list of the name, address, telephone numbers, and all license/registration numbers of the pharmacies involved in centralized prescription dispensing.

The manual shall include policies and procedures for:

- o notifying patients that their prescription may be outsourced to another pharmacy for centralized prescription dispensing and providing the name of that pharmacy.
- o protecting the confidentiality and integrity of patient information.
- o dispensing prescription drug orders when the filled order is not received, or the patient comes in before the order is received.
- o complying with federal and state laws and regulations.
- o operating a continuous quality improvement program for pharmacy services designated to objectively and systematically monitor and evaluate the quality and appropriateness of patient care, pursue opportunities to improve patient care and resolve identified problems.
- o procedure identifying the pharmacist responsible for each aspect of prescription preparation including, but not limited to, the drug regimen review, the initial electronic entry, any changes or modifications to the prescription record or patient profile, and the final check of the completed prescription.
- o identify the pharmacist responsible for counseling the patient pursuant to the requirements of 16.19.4.16 NMAC; and

- annually reviewing the written policies and procedures and documenting such review.

- An application that is not successfully completed within 12 months of the date of initial receipt by the board will be considered withdrawn. For consideration of license issuance, a new application and fee are required.

Records.

- Records may be maintained in an alternative data retention system, such as a data processing system or direct imaging system provided:
  - the records maintained in the alternative system contain all of the information required on the manual record; and
  - the data processing system is capable of producing a hard copy of the record upon request of the board, its' representative, or other authorized local, state, or federal law enforcement or regulatory agencies within 48 hours.

- Each pharmacy shall comply with all the laws and rules relating to the maintenance of records and be able to produce an audit trail showing all prescriptions dispensed by the pharmacy and each pharmacist's or technician's involvement.

- The requesting pharmacy shall maintain records which indicate the date:
  - the request for dispensing was transmitted to the dispensing pharmacy; and
  - the dispensed prescription was received by the requesting pharmacy, including the method of delivery (e.g., private, common, or contract carrier) and the name of the person accepting delivery.

The dispensing pharmacy shall maintain records which indicate:

- o   the date the prescription was shipped to the requesting pharmacy.

- o   the name and address where the prescription was shipped; and

- o   the method of delivery (e.g., private, common, or contract carrier).

16.19.6.29

REMOTE PHARMACY TECHNICIAN DATA ENTRY SITES:

- A New Mexico licensed pharmacy located in New Mexico may employ one or more certified pharmacy technicians for the purpose of data input in remote practice sites provided that all security requirements are met.

- All pharmacy technicians employed to work at a remote data entry practice site must be registered as a certified pharmacy technician with the board and have a minimum of one year experience performing data entry functions as a certified pharmacy tech.

- All remote pharmacy technician data entry sites will operate under a New Mexico licensed pharmacy located in New Mexico under the authority of its pharmacist-in-charge.

- No drug inventory shall be kept at any remote pharmacy technician data entry site and no dispensing shall take place from a remote pharmacy technician data entry site.

- All remote pharmacy technician data entry sites will have a procedure for identifying the pharmacy technician and the pharmacist responsible for each aspect of the prescription preparations.

- All remote pharmacy technician data entry sites will have quality monitoring and improvement programs in place.

Personnel.

- The pharmacist-in-charge shall:

  o provide a written policy and procedure document outlining the operation and security of each remote pharmacy technician data entry site's location; the document shall be available at each practice site.

  o keep a continuously updated list of all remote pharmacy technician data entry sites to include address, phone number and hours of operation for each site; the record shall be retained as part of the records of the licensed pharmacy.

  o is responsible for ensuring that the New Mexico licensed pharmacy and each remote data entry pharmacy technician has entered into a written agreement outlining all conditions and policies governing the operation of the remote site.

  o ensure that all computer equipment used at the remote site is in good working order, provides data protection and complies with all security and HIPAA requirements.

- Data entry pharmacy technician shall:

  - be a certified pharmacy technician registered with the board and reside in New Mexico.

  - have a minimum of one year experience performing data entry functions as a certified pharmacy technician.

  - be trained in the use of all equipment necessary for secure operation of the remote site.

Operations.

- If the remote pharmacy technician data entry sites is located within a home there must be a designated area in which all of the pharmacy technicians work will be performed.

- All computer equipment used at the remote pharmacy technician data entry sites must be able to establish a secure connection which the site is operating. Remote equipment must be configured so that patient information is not stored at the remote site electronically or in printed form.

- Computer equipment may only be used for remote pharmacy technician data entry. No other use of equipment will be allowed.

- Computer equipment must be locked or shut down whenever the pharmacy technician is absent.

- All remote pharmacy technician data entry sites are subject to unannounced inspection by representatives of the New Mexico board of pharmacy during established hours of operation.

- Security.

- Remote pharmacy technician data entry sites shall have adequate security to maintain patient confidentiality.

- Must utilize equipment that prevents unauthorized storage or transfer of patient information.

- If the remote site is in a home, the equipment must be located in a designated area where patient information cannot be viewed by anyone other than the remote pharmacy technician.

16.19.6.30

REPACKAGING AND DISTRIBUTION BY A PHARMACY

- The drug product is not sold or transferred by an entity other than the entity that repackaged such drug product. For purposes of this condition, a sale or transfer does not include administration of a repackaged drug product in a health care setting.

- The drug repackaged is a finished drug product of a prescription drug that is:

  - a non-sterile solid or liquid oral dosage form.

  - approved under Section 505 of the FD&C Act.

  - repackaged by or under the direct supervision of a pharmacist and undergoes a final check by a pharmacist.

  - handled and repackaged in accordance with all applicable USP chapters numbered less than <1000>.

  - assigned a beyond use date in accordance with USP standards.

  - repackaged, stored, and shipped in a way that does not conflict with approved drug product labeling.

  - not adulterated by preparing, packing, or holding the drug product under insanitary conditions; and

  - repackaged into a sealed unit-dose container.

- The repackaged drug product is distributed under the following conditions:

  - by a managing pharmacy for use in an automated drug distribution system to supply medications for patients of a health care facility licensed under 16.19.11 NMAC, or inpatient hospice facility licensed under 16.19.10.12 NMAC, in accordance with 16.19.6.27 NMAC, or emergency kit.

- o to a correctional facility, licensed by the board under 16.19.10.11 NMAC, for administration to an inmate pursuant to a patient-specific prescription or order.

- o to a clinic licensed by the board under 16.19.10.11 NMAC, and under the same ownership as the repackaging pharmacy, for administration to a patient of the clinic pursuant to a patient-specific prescription or order.

- All units of repackaged medication must be labeled with the following information:
  - o name, address, and telephone number of repackaging pharmacy, unless the repackaged drug is used in an automated drug distribution system in accordance with 16.19.6.27 NMAC.
  - o name, strength, and quantity of the drug.
  - o lot number or control number.
  - o name of manufacturer.
  - o beyond use date.
  - o date drug was repackaged.
  - o name or initials of repackage; and
  - o federal caution label, if applicable.

- A record of drugs repackaged must be maintained, and include the following:
  - o date of repackaging.
  - o name and strength of drug.
  - o manufacturer assigned drug lot number, and expiration date.
  - o name of drug manufacturer.
  - o assigned beyond-use date and lot number or control number.

- o total number of dosage units (tabs, caps) repackaged.

- o quantity per each repackaged unit container.

- o number of dosage units wasted; and

- o initials of repackager, and of pharmacist performing final check.

- Records as required by the Pharmacy Act including the Drug, Device, and Cosmetic Act; the Controlled Substance Act; and board regulations shall be maintained.

16.19.7.11

DRUG DISTRIBUTION AND CONTROL:

- In hospitals where there is not a pharmacy, prelabeled, prepackaged medications shall be stored in and distributed from a drug storage area or automated medication management system, which is under the supervision of a pharmacist.

- The pharmacist-in-charge shall have the responsibility for the procurement and storage of all drugs.

- All medications, with the exception of those for emergency use, shall be issued for inpatients use pursuant to the review of the physician's order or direct copy thereof, prior to dispensing. If the pharmacy is closed when the order is written, the pharmacist shall review the order within 24 hours.

- A medication profile for all inpatients and outpatients shall be maintained and used. The medication profile shall serve as the distribution record for inpatient medications. Dangerous drug distribution records, for inpatient use, must include the following information:
  - o the patient's name and room (or bed) number.

- the name, strength, quantity, and dosage form of the drug distributed.

- the name of the technician filling the drug order and pharmacist responsible for checking the technician's work; or

- the name of the pharmacist or pharmacist intern filling the drug order.

- the date filled; and

- the date and amount of unwanted/ unused drug returned to the pharmacy stock.

- records for schedule II-controlled substances must be kept separate; and

- schedule III-V must be kept separate or if stored with non-controlled records, readily retrievable.

- Floor stock dangerous drug distribution records must include the following:

  - name, strength, dosage form, and quantity of the drug distributed.

  - date of filling.

  - a name of technician filling the drug order and the supervising pharmacist; or

  - the name of the pharmacist or pharmacist intern filling the drug order.

  - the destination location of the drug in the hospital; and

  - the date and quantity of unwanted/ unused drug returned to the pharmacy's stock.

  - schedule II controlled substance records must be kept separate from all other records; and schedule IV-controlled substance records must either be kept separate from other non-controlled substances records or are readily retrievable.

- Dangerous drug distribution records, inpatient and floor stock, and medication profiles may be stored electronically if such system is capable of producing a printout of all the required information and the information is retrievable within 72 hours upon demand. The pharmacist stating that it is a true and accurate record must certify the printout. Hospitals utilizing automated drug distribution must comply with Subsection M of 16.19.7.11 NMAC in lieu of the above. Hospital pharmacies are subject to all applicable state and federal record keeping requirements when a prescription from a licensed practitioner is filled.

- A distribution system for controlled substances shall be maintained including perpetual inventory of all schedules II-controlled substances. All schedule II-controlled substances that are stored in the pharmacy will be kept in a locked storage area in the pharmacy.

- Drug storage and preparation areas within the facility shall be the responsibility of the pharmacist-in-charge. All areas shall be inspected on a monthly basis and documented by a pharmacist, intern, or technician.

- All pharmacy preparations of sterile products shall be performed in accordance with the sterile products regulations, 16.19.36 NMAC.

- Floor stock drugs, including those issued from automated medication management systems, shall be limited to drugs for emergency use and routinely used items as listed in the pharmacy policy and procedure manual and approved by the pharmacy and therapeutics committee. Floor stock drugs shall be supplied in individual doses unless the bulk container cannot be individualized. Dangerous drug floor stock must be reviewed by the pharmacist or pharmacist intern on a routine basis to insure appropriate use.

- Where such committees exist, the pharmacist-in-charge or designated pharmacist shall be a voting member of the pharmacy and therapeutics committee or its equivalent.

- Medications dispensed in the emergency room will be dispensed only by a licensed pharmacist, a licensed pharmacist intern or a licensed practitioner and shall comply with the following:
  - a record shall be kept of all medications dispensed from the emergency room of a hospital; the record shall include:

- the date the drug was dispensed.

- name and address of the patient.

- name of the prescribing physician.

- the name of the drug.

- the strength of the drug.

- the quantity of drug dispensed.

- initials of the person recording the information if not a physician.

o a separate record shall be kept for schedule II-controlled substances.

o the following will be recorded in the patient's medical chart:

- the name of the drug(s) prescribed.

- the strength of the drug.

- the quantity of the drug dispensed.

o when medications are prescribed by the physician and dispensed to the patient in the emergency room of the hospital the dispensing label shall contain the following information:

- the name of the patient.

- the name of the prescribing physician.

- name of the drug.

- strength of the drug.

- quantity of the drug.

- name and address of the hospital.

- date the drug is dispensed.

- directions for use.

- expiration date of medication.

Automated Pharmacy Systems.

General Statement:

- Automated devices for storage and distribution of floor stock or patient profile drugs or both, shall be limited to licensed health care facilities and shall comply with all the following provisions. Written policies and procedures, approved by the appropriate health care facility committee, shall be in place to ensure safety, accuracy, security, and patient confidentiality. Personnel allowed access to an automated dispensing device shall have a confidential access code that records the identity and electronic signature of the person accessing the device.

Security/Access:

- The control of access to the automated device must be controlled by the pharmacist-in-charge. Proper identification and access control, including electronic passwords or other coded identification, must be limited and authorized by the pharmacist-in-charge. The pharmacist-in-charge must be able to stop or change access at any time. The pharmacist-in-charge must maintain a current and retrievable list of all persons who have access and the limits of that access. Review of user access reports shall be conducted at least quarterly as established by policy and procedures to ensure that persons who are no longer employed at the facility do not have access to the system.

Records:

- The records kept by the automated drug delivery system must comply with all state, federal, and board requirements. Records must be maintained by the pharmacy and be readily retrievable. Records may be retained in hard copy, or an alternative data retention system may be used where current technology allows.

Automated Drug Distribution:

- An automated medication management system shall be under the control of the pharmacist-in-charge. If used for storage and dispensing of doses scheduled for administration, there shall be a procedure by which orders for a drug are reviewed and approved by the pharmacist before the drug may be withdrawn from the automated dispensing device. There shall be written procedures for downtime in the event of system malfunction or otherwise inoperable. A downtime log shall be maintained and include:

  - date of transaction.

  - patient.

  - drug/dose.

  - quantity of transaction.

  - nurse signature.

  - beginning count.

  - ending count.

  - wasted amount.
  - witness signature, if needed; and
  - prescriber (for controlled substances only).

Quality Assurance:

- The pharmacist-in-charge shall be responsible for developing and implementing a quality assurance program which monitors total system performance. Quality monitors shall include:

- the proper loading/refilling of the device, including proof of delivery.

- the proper removal, return or waste of drugs.

- processes for recording, resolution, and reporting of discrepancies; and

- processes for conducting periodic audits to assure compliance with policies and procedures.

Records: Transaction records:

- At the time of any event involving the contents of the automated device, the device shall automatically produce on demand, a written or electronic record showing:

  - the date and time of transaction.

  - the type of transaction.

  - the name, strength, and quantity of medication.

  - the name of the patient for whom the drug was ordered.

  - the name or identification code (electronic signature) of the person making the transaction.

  - the name of the attending, admitting or prescribing practitioner; and

  - the identity of the device accessed.

- Delivery Records: A delivery record shall be generated on demand for all drugs filled into an automated dispensing device which shall include:

  - date.

  - drug name.

  - dosage form

  - strength.

  - quantity.

41

- identity of device; and

- name or initials of the person filling the automated dispensing device.

Filling:

- There shall be policies and procedures in place, utilizing either manual, bar coding or other electronic processing means of item identities as current technology allows, to ensure pharmacist verification of accuracy in the filling and refilling of the automated device. A delivery record of medications filled into an automated pharmacy system shall be maintained and shall include identification of the person filling the device.

Labeling/Packaging:

- Drugs filled into automated dispensing devices shall be in manufacturers' sealed, original packaging or in repackaged containers in compliance with the requirements of the board regulations relating to packaging and labeling.

Outsourcing of Pharmaceutical Services:

- A hospital pharmacy may contract or enter into an agreement with another licensed pharmacy/pharmacist to provide pharmaceuticals and/or other pharmacist services under the following conditions:
  - the contract pharmacy is licensed by the board of pharmacy.
  - the pharmacist providing the services by the contracted pharmacy shall be licensed as a pharmacist in this state.
  - the contract is incorporated into the pharmacy's policy and procedure manual and complies with the requirements of 16.19.7 NMAC.

42

- o the contracted pharmacy/pharmacist must have complete access to the patient's profile in order to perform a drug regimen review.

- o the contracted pharmacy/pharmacist must have access to the licensed practitioners of the hospital.

- o records of all pharmaceuticals transferred from the contracted pharmacy to the hospital pharmacy comply with the requirements.

- o documentation of the services provided by the contracted pharmacy/pharmacist.

CONSULTANT PHARMACIST:

- Any facility licensed as a clinic by the board which does not employ a staff pharmacist must engage the services of a consultant pharmacist, whose duties and responsibilities are described in Subsection C of 16.19.4.11 NMAC.

- The consultant pharmacist shall wear an identification badge listing his name and job title while on duty in the clinic.

PHARMACY TECHNICIANS AND SUPPORT PERSONNEL:

- Pharmacy technicians, working in a clinic under the supervision of the pharmacist, may perform activities associated with the preparation and distribution of medications, including prepackaging medications and the filling of a prescription or medication order. These activities may include counting, pouring, labeling and reconstituting medications.

- The pharmacist shall ensure that the pharmacy technician has completed the initial training required in Subsection A of 16.19.22.9 NMAC.

- A written record of the initial training and education will be maintained by the clinic pursuant to requirements of Subsection C of 16.19.22.9 NMAC.

- The permissible ratio of pharmacy technicians to pharmacists on duty is to be determined by the pharmacist in charge or consultant pharmacist.

- Support personnel may perform clerical duties associated with clinic pharmacy operations, including computer data entry, typing of labels, processing of orders for stock, duties associated with maintenance of inventory and dispensing records.

- The pharmacist is responsible for the actions of personnel; allowing actions outside the limits of the regulations shall constitute unprofessional conduct on the part of the pharmacist.

- Name tags including job title, shall be required of all personnel while on duty in the clinic.

PROCUREMENT OR RECEIPT OF DANGEROUS DRUGS:

- The system of procurement for all drugs shall be the responsibility of the pharmacist.

- Records of receipt of dangerous drugs and inventories of controlled substances shall be maintained as required by the Drug, Device and Cosmetic Act 26-1-16 and the Controlled Substances Act 30-31-16 and board of pharmacy regulation 16.19.20 NMAC.

CLINIC DISPENSING OR DISTRIBUTING:

- Drugs shall be dispensed or distributed only to clinic patients on the order of a licensed practitioner of the clinic.

- The clinic practitioner shall record the prescribed drug therapy on the patient medical record indicating the name, strength, quantity, and directions for use of the prescribed drug. This information shall be initialed or signed by the practitioner. A separate prescription form in addition to the medical record may be used.

The prescription order may then be prepared by the practitioner, pharmacist, or technician under the supervision of the pharmacist and a dispensing label affixed to the dispensing unit of each drug. The following information shall appear on the label affixed to the dispensing unit.

- Name of patient.

- Name of prescriber.

- Date of dispensing.

- Directions for use.

- Name, strength, and quantity of the drug.

- Expiration date.

- Name, address, and phone number of the clinic.

- Prescription number, if applicable.

- The pharmacist or practitioner must then provide a final check of the dispensing unit and sign or initial the prescription or dispensing record.

- Refill prescription orders must also be entered on the patient's medical record and the dispensing record.

PATIENT COUNSELING:

- Each clinic licensed by the board shall develop and provide to the board policies and procedures addressing patient counseling which are at least equivalent to the requirements of Subsection F of 16.19.4.16 NMAC.

- If the consultant pharmacist is absent at the time of dispensing or distribution of a prescription from clinic drug stock to a clinic patient, the patient shall be provided written information when appropriate on side effects, interactions, and precautions concerning the drug or device provided. The clinic shall make the consultant pharmacist's phone number available to patients for consultation on drugs provided by the clinic.

DISPENSING RECORDS:

- A record shall be kept of the dangerous drugs dispensed indicating the date the drug was dispensed, name and address of the patient, the name of the prescriber, and the quantity and strength of the drug dispensed. The individual recording the information and the pharmacist or clinic practitioner who is responsible for dispensing the medication shall initial the record.

SAMPLE DRUGS:

- Samples of medications which are legend drugs, or which have been restricted to the sale on prescription by the New Mexico board of pharmacy are subject to all the record keeping, storage and labeling requirements for prescription drugs as defined by NMSA 26-1-16 and other applicable state and federal laws.

DISPOSITION OF UNWANTED OR OUTDATED DRUGS:

- The pharmacist shall be responsible for removal of recalled, outdated, unwanted or otherwise unusable drugs from the clinic inventory.

- Options for disposal are destruction under the supervision of the pharmacist or return to the legitimate source of supply.

16.19.15.20

CONSULTANT PHARMACIST:

- Any retail distributor licensed by the Board to dispense veterinary prescription drugs is required to have a consultant pharmacist.

- Consultant pharmacists to retail distributors of veterinary prescription products are required to visit the facility every other month. Consultant pharmacists to retail distributors of veterinary prescription products that do not dispense controlled substances are required to visit the licensed facility quarterly.

- The consultant pharmacist shall maintain a log or record of all visits and activities at the retail distributor of veterinary prescription products. That record shall document at least the following:
  - the date of the annual review of the Policy and Procedure Manual required by 16.19.4.11 NMAC.
  - prescriptions are in a consecutively numbered file.
  - all procurement, distribution by prescription wholesalers, and disposition records are maintained for at least 3 years.
  - all inventory of dangerous drugs is stored in an area not accessible to unauthorized persons.
  - all dangerous drugs are stored according to USP/NF requirements with adequate ventilation, lighting, temperature controls and refrigeration.
  - the facility is in compliance with all State and Federal laws and regulations for the procurement, storage and dispensing of dangerous drugs; and

o   orientation and training of all facility employees, who have access to the dangerous drugs, to the legal requirements of dangerous drugs and to the Policy and Procedure Manual of the facility.

16.19.16.8

DISTRIBUTION OF PHARMACEUTICAL SAMPLES:

- No person regulated by this Board including a person acting as principal or agent (detail person) for a manufacturer, wholesaler, or distributor shall buy, sell, trade, barter or exchange, or offer to buy, sell, trade, barter or exchange:

- Pharmaceutical product samples.

- Pharmaceutical products sold for export only.

- Pharmaceuticals purchased by hospitals, and/or clinics, including agencies of state and local governments for the exclusive use of those institutions and not intended for resale.

- Pharmaceutical products donated or supplied at reduced prices to charitable institutions in the United States or abroad for their own institutional use.

- Complementary pharmaceutical product trade packages.

- Sales otherwise permitted by law to affiliated corporations in furtherance of a planned, integrated approach to the delivery of health care within a health care corporate structure and sales by a bona fide group purchasing arrangement to members are not subject to 16.19.16.8 NMAC nor are emergency borrowing/lending between licensed health care facilities.

- Violations of these regulations is grounds for revocation of licenses or permits issued by the Board of Pharmacy.

REGISTRATION REQUIREMENTS:

Persons required to register manufacture - term includes repackages.

- distributors - term includes wholesale drug distributors.

- dispensers - pharmacies, hospital pharmacies, clinics (both health and veterinarian);

- practitioners - includes a physician, doctor of oriental medicine, dentist, physician assistant, certified nurse practitioner, clinical nurse specialist, certified nurse-midwife, veterinarian, pharmacist, pharmacist clinician, certified registered nurse anesthetists, psychologists, chiropractic examiner, euthanasia technicians or other person licensed or certified to prescribe and administer drugs that are subject to the Controlled Substances Act. Practitioners, excluding veterinarians, must register with the New Mexico prescription monitoring program in conjunction with their controlled substance registration.

- scientific investigators or researchers.

- analytical laboratories and chemical analysis laboratories.

- teaching institutes.

- special projects and demonstrations which bear directly on misuse or abuse of controlled substances - may include public agencies, institutions of higher education and private organizations.

- registration waiver: an individual licensed practitioner (e.g., intern, resident, staff physician, mid-level practitioner) who is an agent or employee of a hospital or clinic, licensed by the board, may, when acting in the usual course of employment or business, order-controlled substances, for administration to the patients of the facility, under controlled substance registration of the hospital or clinic in which he or she is employed provided that:

o   the ordering of controlled substances for administration, to the patients of the hospital or clinic, is in the usual course of professional practice and the hospital or clinic authorizes the practitioner to order controlled substances for the administration to its patients under its state-controlled substance registration.

o   the hospital or clinic has verified with the practitioner's licensing board that the practitioner is permitted to order controlled substances within the state.

o   the practitioner acts only within their scope of employment in that hospital or clinic.

o   the hospital or clinic maintains a current list of practitioners given such authorization and includes the practitioner's full name, date of birth, professional classification and license number, and home and business addresses and phone numbers.

o   the list is available at all times to board inspectors, the DEA, law enforcement and health professional licensing boards; and

o   the hospital or clinic shall submit a current list of authorized practitioners with each hospital or clinic-controlled substance renewal application.

16.19.20.9

REGISTRATION AND EXPIRATION DATES:

- Any person who is required to be registered and who is not registered may apply for registration at any time.

- In December 1982 all registrant renewal dates will be assigned to one of 12 groups which shall correspond to the months of the year. Thereafter, any person who first registers will also be assigned to one of the 12 groups. Expiration date of the registration of all individuals or businesses within any group will be the last day of the month designated for that group.

Renewal date will be within 30 days of the date shown on the registration permit and will expire on that date if not renewed by the registrant.

- Renewal applications will be mailed to the physical, mailing, or electronic address indicated on the application on file or as amended by change of address supplied by the registrant to the board of pharmacy.

16.19.20.11

APPLICATION FORMS:

- Application forms may be obtained from the board of pharmacy, Albuquerque, New Mexico.

16.19.20.12

SCHEDULES:

- Applications shall designate the schedule of controlled substances and whether the application is for narcotic or non-narcotic in schedules I through V.

16.19.20.13

SEPARATE REGISTRATION OF EACH PRINCIPAL PLACE OF BUSINESS:

- Separate registration is required for each principal place of business or professional practice with the address indicated on the application if drugs are dispensed or distributed from the different locations. NOTE: This does not include warehouse storage areas; office used by agents for soliciting which contain no controlled substances other than samples, physician's office where controlled substances are prescribed but not administered or otherwise dispensed.

16.19.20.14

INFORMATION REQUIRED:

- The board shall register an applicant to manufacture or distribute controlled substances unless it determines that the issuance of that registration would be inconsistent with the public interest. In determining the public interest, the board may consider the following factors from information listed on the application:
  - maintenance of effective controls against diversion of controlled substances.
  - compliance with applicable state and local law.
  - any convictions of the applicant under any federal or state laws relating to any controlled substance.
  - past experience in the manufacture or distribution of controlled substances, and the existence in the applicant's establishment of effective controls against diversion.
  - furnishing by the applicant of false or fraudulent material in any application filed under the Controlled Substances Act.
  - suspension or revocation of the applicant's federal registration to manufacture, distribute or dispense controlled substances as authorized by federal law; and
  - any other factors relevant to and consistent with the public health and safety.
- Each application shall include all information as required on the application form, including but not limited to a current DEA registration and professional license, and shall be signed by
- the applicant.

16.19.20.15

FACILITY INSPECTION:

- The board of pharmacy may direct the drug inspector to inspect the facilities prior to approval of any application for security provision and other applicable standards as required by the Controlled Substances Act.

16.19.20.16

PROCEDURE SUMMARY, RESEARCH:

- A scientific investigator or research applicant shall submit a summary of procedures indicating the nature, extent and duration of such research. The summary shall also include the names of individuals engaged in the project (other than those exempt under the Controlled Substances Act) the name or names of the substances to be used in the research project, the adequacy of safeguards against diversion of the controlled substance(s) to be used, source of supply of controlled substance(s) if applicable, and evidence of FDA and DEA approval and registration if registered by the federal agencies.

16.19.20.17

ANALYTICAL LABORATORIES:

- Analytical laboratory applicants shall submit application on the form provided by the board. All applicable questions on the application shall be filled in and signed by the person in charge of the facility.

- Quantities of controlled substances in possession of analytical laboratories shall be limited to such quantities as required for reference standards, assays or other scientific purposes

16.19.20.18

EXEMPTION OF LAW ENFORCEMENT OFFICIALS:

- Registration is waived for the following persons:
- Any officer or employee of the state or federal customs agency, the state police, or any enforcement officer of any political subdivision of the state, who is engaged in the enforcement of any federal, state and local law relating to controlled substances and is duly authorized to possess controlled substances in the course of his official duties.
- Any official exempted by this section may procure any controlled substance in the course of an inspection pursuant to Section 31 of the Controlled Substances Act or in the course of any criminal investigation involving the person from whom the substance was procured.
- Laboratory personnel, when acting in the scope of their official duties, are also exempt from registration under the Controlled Substances Act.

16.19.20.19

MODIFICATION, TRANSFER AND TERMINATION OF REGISTRATION:

- Modification of a registration to authorize additional controlled substances may be made by filing an application in the same number as an application for a new registration. No fee shall be required for such modification.

- Registration shall terminate if and when a registrant dies, discontinues business or professional practice, has his professional license revoked or suspended, no longer possesses a DEA registration or has had his DEA registration revoked or suspended, or changes his name or address as shown on the registration. In such instances, the registrant or his estate shall notify the board of pharmacy promptly of such fact and return certificate of registration to the board within 30 days.

- Inventories and records of controlled substances listed in schedules II, III, IV and V shall be maintained either separately from all other records or in such form that the information required is readily retrievable from ordinary business records of the registrant.

- In the event of a change in name or address the person shall file an application in the same number as an application for modification of a registration. No fee shall be required for such modification.

- Registration under the Controlled Substances Act shall not be transferable.

16.19.20.20

INVENTORY RECORDS:

- All registrants are required to keep inventory and procurement records.

- All registrants shall comply with the following inventory requirements: schedule I, II, III, IV and V initial, annual, newly controlled substances, change in pharmacist in charge, and transfer of pharmacy ownership.

- All registrants shall conduct an initial inventory of all controlled substances on hand on the date they first engage in controlled substances activity. In the event a registrant commences business with no controlled substances on hand, he/she shall record this fact on the initial inventory.

- The annual inventory date shall be May 1 or on the registrant's regular general physical inventory date, provided that the registrant shall notify the board of pharmacy of the set alternate annual inventory date. The actual taking of the inventory should not vary more than four days before or after the annual inventory date (May 1 or set alternate date).

- On the effective date that a substance is added to any schedule of controlled substances, which substance was, immediately prior to that date, not listed on any schedule, every registrant who possesses that substance shall take an inventory of all stock of the substance on hand and file this record with the other inventory records as required.

- Upon the change of a pharmacist-in-charge, an inventory of all controlled substances shall be taken within 72 hours, by the new pharmacist-in-charge.

- Upon transfer of ownership of a pharmacy, an inventory of all controlled substances shall be taken by the pharmacist-in-charge.

- The inventory shall include:

    o the date.

    o time taken (i.e., opening or close of business).

    o drug name.

    o the drug strength.

    o the drug form (e.g., tablet, capsule, etc.).

    o the number of units or volume.

    o the total quantity. A commercial container which has been opened shall be the exact count or measure of substances listed in schedule I or schedule II. If the substance is listed in schedule III, IV or V, he shall make an estimated count or measure of the contents, unless the container holds more than 1,000 tablets or capsules in which case the count must be exact.

- o expired or unusable controlled substances shall be documented as such, and inventoried.

- The name, address and DEA registration number of the registrant.

- The signature of the person or persons responsible for taking the inventory.

16.19.20.21

INVENTORY RECORDS OF MANUFACTURERS AND REPACKAGERS:

- Manufacturers and repackages inventory records shall contain the following information:
- Finished form:
    - o name of substance.
    - o each finished form of the substance (10 milligram tablet, etc.)
    - o the number of units or volume of each finished form in each commercial container (100 tablet bottle, etc.)
    - o the number of commercial containers of each such finished form.
- Controlled substances not included above such as damaged, defective impure substances awaiting a disposal giving total quantity and the name of the substance. A statement of reason for the substance being included in this category.

16.19.20.23

INVENTORY REQUIREMENTS - RESEARCH:

- Research registrant shall include in his inventory the name of the substance, each finished form of the substance, the number of units or volume of each finished form in each commercial container (100 tablet bottle, etc.) and the number of commercial containers of each such finished form.

- A commercial container which has been opened shall be the exact count or measure of substances listed in schedule I or schedule II. If the substance is listed in schedule III, IV or V, he shall make an estimated count or measure of the contents, unless the container holds more than 1,000 tablets or capsules in which case the count must be exact.

16.19.20.25

CONTROLLED SUBSTANCES INVENTORIES AND RECORDS:

- Pharmacies, hospitals, clinics and practitioners who dispense controlled substances shall maintain inventories and records of controlled substances listed in schedules II and II-N separately from all of the other prescription records.

- "Readily retrievable" means records kept in such a manner as to be easily separated out from all other records in a reasonable time or records are kept on which certain items are redlined, starred or in some manner are visually identifiable apart from other items appearing on the record.

16.19.20.41

PRESCRIPTIONS:

- A prescription for a controlled substance may be issued for a legitimate medical purpose by an individual practitioner acting in the usual course of his professional practice, and who is registered under the Controlled Substances Act. The responsibility for the proper prescribing and dispensing of controlled substances is upon the prescribing practitioner, but a corresponding responsibility rests with the pharmacist who fills the prescription.

- A prescription may not be issued in order for a practitioner to obtain controlled substances for supplying the practitioner for the purpose of general dispensing to patients.

- A prescription may not be issued for the dispensing of narcotic drugs listed in any schedule to a narcotic dependent person for the sole purpose of continuing his dependence upon such drugs, unless all the following conditions are met:

  - the narcotic controlled drug is in Schedule III, IV, or V and is approved by the Food and Drug Administration specifically for use in maintenance or detoxification treatment; and

  - the prescribing practitioner meets all state and federal requirements to prescribe the narcotic for maintenance or detoxification treatment (e.g. DATA waived practitioner; 21 CFR 1301.28 or successor regulation).

16.19.20.42

PRESCRIPTION REQUIREMENTS:

- All prescriptions for controlled substances shall be dated as of, and signed on, the day when issued and shall bear the full name and address of the patient, the drug name, strength, dosage form, quantity prescribed, directions for use, and the name, address and registration number of the practitioner. Information on the prescription may be added or clarified by the pharmacist after consultation with the practitioner. A practitioner may sign a paper prescription in the same manner as he would sign a check or legal document (e.g., J.H. Smith or John H. Smith). Where an oral order is not permitted, paper prescriptions must be written with ink or indelible pencil, typewriter, or printed on a computer printer and shall be manually signed by the practitioner. A computer-generated prescription that is printed out or faxed by the practitioner must be manually signed.

- Electronic prescriptions shall be created and signed using an application that meets the requirements of Part 1311 of the Code of Federal Regulations. An individual practitioner will sign and transmit electronic prescriptions for controlled substances in a manner that meets all of the requirements of Part 1306.08 of the Code of Federal Regulations.

- Effective April 1, 2021 all controlled substance prescriptions must be electronically transmitted ("Electronic Prescriptions for Controlled Substances," EPCS) except:
    - o for patients residing in an intermediate care, skilled nursing or correctional facility.
    - o for patients enrolled in hospice.
    - o for an animal by a licensed veterinarian.
    - o a prescription dispensed by a federal facility not subject to state regulation (e.g. department of veteran affairs, Indian health services, military bases);

- a prescription requiring information that makes electronic transmission impractical, such as complicated or lengthy directions for use or attachments, or new medications not yet in electronic system.

- for compounded prescriptions.

- for prescriptions issued during a temporary technical or electronic failure at the practitioner's or pharmacy's location.

- for prescriptions issued in an emergency pursuant to federal law and rules of the board.

- for prescriptions issued in response to a public health emergency where a non-patient specific prescription would be permitted.

- under extenuating circumstance, not inconsistent with federal law and where the practitioner communicates directly with the pharmacist. The pharmacist, using professional judgment, may accept the non-EPCS and is responsible for ensuring documentation of the circumstance in the prescription record; and that the prescription is otherwise in compliance with state and federal law and rules.

- Unless otherwise specified, a pharmacist who receives a written, oral, or facsimile prescription

  - shall not be required to verify that the prescription is subject to an exemption and may dispense a prescription drug pursuant to an otherwise valid written, oral, or facsimile prescription.

- A prescription that falls under an exception to the EPCS requirement may be transmitted to a pharmacy in one of the following ways:

- A prescription for a schedule II controlled substance may be transmitted by the practitioner or the practitioner's agent to a pharmacy via facsimile equipment, provided the original written, signed prescription is presented to the pharmacist for review prior to the actual dispensing of the controlled substance, except as noted in Paragraphs 2, 3 and 4 of this Subsection. The original prescription shall be maintained in accordance with 16.19.20.31 NMAC.

- A prescription prepared in accordance with Subsection A of 16.19.20.42 NMAC written for a schedule II narcotic substance to be compounded for the direct administration to a patient by parenteral, intravenous, intramuscular, or subcutaneous infusion may be transmitted by the practitioner or the practitioner's agent to the parenteral products pharmacy by facsimile. The facsimile serves as the original written prescription for purposes of this paragraph, and it shall be maintained in accordance with 16.19.20.31 NMAC.

- A prescription prepared in accordance with Subsection A of 16.19.20.42 NMAC written for a schedule II substance for a resident of a long-term care facility may be transmitted by the practitioner or the practitioner's agent to the dispensing pharmacy by facsimile. The facsimile serves as the original written prescription for purposes of this sub-section, and it shall be maintained in accordance with 16.19.20.31 NMAC.

- A prescription prepared in accordance with Subsection A of 16.19.20.41 NMAC written for a schedule II narcotic substance for a patient enrolled in a hospice program certified by Medicare under title XVIII or licensed by the state may be transmitted by the practitioner or the practitioner's agent to the dispensing pharmacy by facsimile. The practitioner or the practitioner's agent will note on the prescription that the patient is a hospice patient. The facsimile serves as the original written prescription for purposes of this sub-section, and it shall be maintained in accordance with 16.19.20.31 NMAC.

- A pharmacist may dispense directly a controlled substance listed in schedule III, IV, or V which is a prescription drug as determined under the New Mexico Drug Device and

Cosmetic Act, only pursuant to either a written prescription signed by a practitioner or a facsimile of a written, signed prescription transmitted by the practitioner or the practitioner's agent to the pharmacy or pursuant to an oral prescription made by an individual practitioner and promptly reduced to written form by the pharmacist containing all information required for a prescription except the signature of the practitioner. A telephone order for a new therapy for an opiate listed in schedule III, IV, or V shall not exceed a 10-day supply, based on the directions for use, unless a written prescription is on file at this pharmacy from any practitioner for the same opiate within the past six months. A telephone order for this new opiate therapy may not be refilled.

- A pharmacy employee shall verify the identity of the patient or the patient's representative who is receiving any prescription for a controlled substance listed in schedule II, III, IV, or V before it is released. Acceptable identification means a current state issued driver's license, including photo, or other current government issued photo identification of the person presenting said identification. The identification type (e.g. driver's license, identification card, passport, etc.), number, name imprinted on that identification, and state must be recorded. Exceptions are, a new controlled substance prescription filled for a patient known to the pharmacist or pharmacist intern, whose identification has already been documented in a manner determined by a written policy developed by the pharmacist-in-charge; a controlled substance prescription filled for home delivery; or a controlled substance prescription filled for and delivered to a licensed facility.

16.19.20.43

PRESCRIPTIONS NOT TO BE REFILLED:

- Prescriptions for schedule II drugs may not be refilled.

16.19.20.44

REFILL PROCEDURE:

- Each refilling of a schedule III, IV or V controlled substance prescription shall be entered in prescription record, indicating the amount dispensed, if less than the amount called for on the prescription, the date of refill and the initials of the pharmacist dispensing the substance.

16.19.20.45

PRESCRIPTION FILL AND REFILL REQUIREMENTS:

- Prescriptions for any controlled substance shall not be filled more than six months after the date of issue.
- Controlled substance prescriptions dispensed directly to a patient shall not be refilled before seventy-five percent of the prescription days' supply has passed, unless the practitioner authorizes the early refill, which must be documented by the pharmacist.
- Controlled substance prescriptions delivered to a patient indirectly (as mail order) to a patient shall not be refilled before sixty-six percent of a 90-day supply has passed or fifty percent of a 30 day supply has passed, unless the practitioner authorizes the early refill, which must be documented by the pharmacist.

- Prescriptions for schedule III, IV, or V controlled substances shall not be filled or refilled more than six months after the date of issue or be refilled more than five times unless renewed by the practitioner and a new prescription is placed in the pharmacy files.

16.19.20.46

PRESCRIPTION - PARTIALLY FILLED:

- A prescription for a controlled substance in schedule II may be partially filled if:
  - the total quantity dispensed in all partial fillings does not exceed the total quantity prescribed.
  - the partial fill amount is recorded on the written prescription or in the electronic prescription record; and
  - the remaining portions shall be filled not later than 30 days after the date on which the prescription is issued.
- A prescription for a controlled substance in schedule II initially filled later than 30 days after the date issued may be partially filled if.
  - the pharmacist is unable to dispense the total quantity prescribed.
  - the partial fill amount is recorded on the written prescription or in the electronic prescription record.
  - the remaining portion is filled within 72 hours of the partial filling; and
  - the pharmacist notifies the prescribing physician if the remaining portion cannot be filled within the 72-hour period. No further quantity may be supplied beyond 72 hours without a new prescription.

- Partial filling of a prescription for schedule III, IV or V shall be recorded in the same manner as a refill, providing the total quantity of partial filling does not exceed the total quantity prescribed and no dispensing occurs after six months from date of prescription.

- A prescription for a schedule II-controlled substance written for a patient in a long-term care facility (LTCF) or for a patient with a medical diagnosis documenting a terminal illness may be filled in partial quantities, to include individual dosage units.

- If there is any question whether a patient may be classified as having a terminal illness, the pharmacist shall contact the practitioner prior to partially filling the prescription. Both the pharmacist and the prescribing practitioner have a corresponding responsibility to assure that the controlled substance is for a terminally ill patient. The pharmacist shall record on the prescription whether the patient is "terminally ill" or an "LTCF patient".

- A prescription that is partially filled and does not contain the notation "terminally ill" or LTCF patient" shall be deemed to have been filled in violation of this regulation. For each partial filling, the dispensing pharmacist shall record on the back of the prescription (or on appropriate record, uniformly maintained, and readily retrievable) the date of the partial filling, quantity dispensed, remaining quantity authorized to be dispensed and the identification of the dispensing pharmacist.

- The total quantity of schedule II-controlled substances dispensed in all partial fillings shall not exceed the total quantity prescribed. Schedule II prescriptions, for patients in a LTCF or patients with a medical diagnosis documenting a terminal illness, shall be valid for a period not to exceed 60 days from the issue date unless sooner terminated by the discontinuance of medication.

16.19.20.47

EMERGENCY DISPENSING:

- Emergency dispensing of schedule II-controlled substances. "Emergency situation" means the prescribing physician determines:
  - that immediate administration of a controlled substance is necessary for proper treatment of the intended patient.
  - that no appropriate alternative treatment is available, including administration of a drug which is not a controlled substance under schedule II; and
  - that it is not reasonably possible for the prescribing practitioner to provide an electronically prescribed or written prescription to be presented to the person dispensing the substance prior to the dispensing.
- A pharmacy may dispense a schedule II-controlled substance in the above instance only if he receives oral authorization of a practitioner or authorization via facsimile machine and provided:
  - the quantity prescribed is limited to the amount needed to treat the patient during the emergency period.
  - the pharmacist shall reduce the prescription to a written form, and it contains all information required of a schedule II-controlled substance prescription except the signature of the prescribing practitioner.
  - the prescribing physician, within seven days after authorization of the emergency dispensing, shall furnish a written, signed prescription to the pharmacist. The signed

prescription shall have written on the face "AUTHORIZATION FOR

EMERGENCY DISPENSING" and the date of the oral order or facsimile order.

- o the signed prescription shall be attached to the oral emergency prescription order or

  the facsimile emergency prescription order and be filed as other schedule II

  prescriptions.

- In the event the prescribing physician fails to deliver a signed written prescription to the

  pharmacist, within the seven days period, the pharmacist shall notify the nearest DEA office,

  and the board of pharmacy.

16.19.20.64

CONTROLLED SUBSTANCE PRECURSORS:

- See 16.19.21 NMAC – Drug Precursors

16.19.20.65

SCHEDULE I:

- Section 30-31-6 NMSA 1978, schedule I shall consist of the following drugs and other

  substances, by whatever name, common or usual name, chemical name or brand name

  designated, listed in this section; OPIOIDS, unless specifically exempt or unless listed in

  another schedule, any of the following opioids, including its isomers, esters, ethers, salts and

  salts of isomers, esters, and ethers, whenever the existence of such isomers, esters, ethers,

  and salts is possible within the specific chemical designation.

16.19.20.66

SCHEDULE II:

- OPIOIDS: Unless specifically excepted or unless in another schedule any of the following opioids, including its isomers, esters, ethers, salts and salts of isomers, esters, and ethers whenever the existence of such isomers, esters, ethers, and salts is possible within the specific chemical designation except dextro and levopropoxyphene.

16.19.20.67

SCHEDULE III:

- Shall consist of drugs and other substances, by whatever official name, common or usual name designated listed in this section.
- NARCOTIC DRUGS: Unless specifically exempt or unless listed in another schedule, any material, compound, mixture or preparation containing limited quantities of the following narcotic drugs, or any salts thereof.
- Not more than one and eight-tenths grams of codeine per 100 milliliters or not more than 90 milligrams per dosage unit, with an equal or greater quantity of an isoquinoline alkaloid of opium.
- Not more than one and eight-tenths grams of codeine per 100 milliliters or not more than 90 milligrams per dosage units, with one or more active nonnarcotic ingredients in recognized therapeutic amounts. Not more than 300 milligrams of dihydrocodeinone per 100 milliliters or not more than 15 milligrams per dosage unit, with a fourfold or greater quantity of an isoquinoline alkaloid of opium.

- Not more than 300 milligrams of dihydrocodeinone per 100 milliliters or not more than 15 milligrams per dosage unit, with one or more active, nonnarcotic ingredients in recognized therapeutic amounts.

- Not more than one and eight-tenths grams of dihydrocodeine per 100 milliliters or not more than 90 milligrams per dosage unit, with one or more active, nonnarcotic ingredients in recognized therapeutic amounts.

- Not more than 300 milligrams of ethylmorphine per 100 milliliters or not more than 15 milligrams per dosage unit, with one or more active, nonnarcotic ingredients in recognized therapeutic amounts.

- Not more than 500 milligrams of opium per 100 milliliters or per 100 grams or not more than 25 milligrams per dosage unit, with one or more active, nonnarcotic ingredients in recognized therapeutic amounts.

- Not more than 50 milligrams of morphine per 100 milliliters or per 100 grams, with one or more active, nonnarcotic ingredients in recognized therapeutic amounts.

- STIMULANTS: Unless specifically exempt or unless listed in another schedule, any material, compound, mixture or preparation which contains any quantity of the following substances having a stimulant effect on the central nervous system.

- Those compounds, mixtures or preparations in dosage unit form containing any stimulant, amphetamine, phenmetrazine or methamphetamine previously exempt, for which the exemption was revoked by FDA Regulation Title 21, Part 308.13, and any other drug of the quantitative composition shown in that regulation for those drugs or which is the same except that it contains a lesser quantity of controlled substances.

16.19.20.68

SCHEDULE IV:

- Shall consist of the drugs and other substances, by whatever official name, common or usual name, chemical name, or brand name designated, listed in this section.

- DEPRESSANTS: Unless specifically exempt or unless listed in another schedule, any material, compound, mixture or preparation which contains any quantity of the following substances, including its salts, isomers, and salts of isomers whenever the existence of such salts, isomers and salts of isomers is possible within the specific chemical designation:

16.19.20.69

SCHEDULE V:

- Narcotic drugs containing non-narcotic active medicinal ingredients. Any compound, mixture, or preparation containing any of the following narcotic drugs, or their salts calculated as the free anhydrous base or alkaloid, in limited quantities as set forth below, which shall include one or more non-narcotic active medicinal ingredients in sufficient proportion to confer upon the compound, mixture, or preparation valuable medicinal qualities other than those possessed by narcotic drugs alone.

- Not more than 200 milligrams of codeine per 100 milliliters or per 100 grams.

- Not more than 100 milligrams of dihydrocodeine per 100 milliliters or per 100 grams.

- Not more than 100 milligrams of ethylmorphine per 100 milliliters or per 100 grams.

- Not more than two and five-tenths milligrams of diphenoxylate and not less than 25 micrograms of atropine sulfate per dosage unit.

- Not more than 100 milligrams of opium per 100 milliliters or per 100 grams.

- Not more than five-tenths milligrams of difenoxin and not less than 25 micrograms of atropine sulfate per dosage unit.

- Stimulants. Unless specifically exempted or excluded or unless listed in another schedule, any material, compound, mixture or preparation which contains any quantity of the following substances having a stimulant effect on the central nervous system, including its salts, isomers and salts of isomers.

- Pyrovalerone.

- Pseudoephedrine as a drug that includes any compound, mixture, or preparation that contains any detectable quantity of pseudoephedrine, its salts or its optical isomers, or salts of its optical isomers. Pursuant to 30-31-10.C the following substances are excluded from schedule V controlled substances: pseudoephedrine products in liquid form including liquid filled gel caps and pseudoephedrine products already classified as dangerous drugs.

- Depressants. Unless specifically exempted or excluded or unless listed in another schedule, any material, compound, mixture, or preparation which contains any quantity of the following substances having a depressant effect on the central nervous system, including its salts:

  - Lacosamide [(R)-2acetoamido-N-benzyl-3-methoxy-propionamide]
  - Pregabalin [(S)-3-(aminomethyl)-5-methylhexanoic acid]
  - Ezogabine [N-[2-amino-4-(4-flurobenzylamino-phenyl]-carbamic acid ethyl ester]
  - Brivaracetam
  - Cenobamate

16.19.21.8

PERSONS REQUIRED TO REGISTER:

- The board shall license an applicant to manufacture, possess, transfer or transport drug precursors unless it determines that the issuance of that license would be inconsistent with the public interest. In determining the public interest, the board may consider the following factors:

  o maintenance of effective controls against diversion of drug precursors into other than legitimate medical, scientific or industrial channels;

  o compliance with applicable state and local law;

  o any conviction of the applicant under federal or state laws relating to any controlled substance or drug precursor;

  o past experience in the manufacturer, possession, transfer or transportation of drug precursors and the existence in the applicant's establishment of effective controls against diversion;

  o furnishing by the applicant of false or fraudulent material in any application filed under the Drug Precursor Act or the Controlled Substances Act;

  o suspension or revocation of the applicant's federal registration to manufacture, distribute or dispense controlled substances or drug precursors as authorized by federal law; and

  o any other factors relevant to and consistent with the public health and safety.

- Licensing under this section does not entitle a licensee to manufacture, possess, transfer or transport drug precursors other than those allowed in the license.

16.19.21.17

EXEMPTION OF LAW ENFORCEMENT OFFICIALS:

- Registration is waived for the following persons:

- Any officer or employee of the state or federal customs agency, the state police, or any enforcement officer of any political subdivision of the state, who is engaged in the enforcement of federal, state and local law relating to drug precursors and is duly authorized to possess drug precursors in the course of his official duties.

- Any official exempted by this section may procure any drug precursor in the course of an inspection pursuant to any section of the Drug Precursor Act or in the course of any criminal investigation involving the person from whom the substance was procured.

- Laboratory personnel, when acting in the scope of his official duties, are also exempt from registration under the Drug Precursor Act.

16.19.21.18

TRANSFER AND TERMINATION OF REGISTRATION:

- Registration shall terminate if and when a registrant dies, discontinues business or professional practice, has his professional license revoked or suspended, or changes his name or address as shown on the registration. In such instance, the registrant or his estate shall notify the Board of Pharmacy promptly of such fact and return certificate of registration to the Board. Inventories and records of drug precursors shall be maintained separately from all other records or in such form that the information is readily retrievable from ordinary business records of the registrant.

- In the event of a change in name or address, the registrant shall file an application in the same manner as an application for a new registration. No fee shall be required for such modification.

- Registration under the Drug Precursor Act is not transferable.

16.19.21.24

DISPOSITION OF DAMAGED, OUTDATED, OR UNWANTED DRUG PRECURSORS:

- Any registrant in possession of any drug precursor and desiring to dispose of such substance must abide by any applicable federal, state, local law or regulation for the destruction of such substance. This destruction must be witnessed by at least one law enforcement officer certified in the State of New Mexico. Appropriate records must be kept of the destruction.

16.19.21.25

DISTRIBUTION UPON TRANSFER OR DISCONTINUANCE OF BUSINESS:

- Upon transfer of a business from one owner to another, the owner may dispose of the drug precursors in the following manner:
  - have the drug precursor destroyed as discussed in 16.19.21.24 NMAC;
  - transfer the drug precursors to the new owner. All records required to be kept by the registrant-transferor with reference to the drug precursors being transferred shall be transferred to the registrant-transferee. Responsibility for the accuracy of records

prior to the date of transfer remains with the transferor, but responsibility for custody and maintenance shall be upon the transferee.

- Upon discontinuance of business, if there are drug precursors which are not transferred to another registrant, these substances shall be handled as unwanted drug precursors under 16.19.21.24 NMAC.

16.19.21.26

SECURITY REQUIREMENTS:

- All applicants and registrants shall provide effective controls and procedures to guard against theft and diversion of drug precursors.

- In evaluating the overall security system of a registrant or applicant, the following factors may be considered:
    - the type of activity;
    - the quantity of drug precursors;
    - the location of premises and the relationship such location plays on security needs;
    - the type of building construction of the facility and the general characteristic of the building;
    - the adequacy of key control systems and/or lock control systems;
    - the extent of unsupervised public access to the facility;
    - the adequacy of supervision over employees having access to storage and distribution areas;
    - the process for handling business guests, visitors, maintenance personnel, and non-employee service personnel;

o the adequacy of the registrant's or applicant's system for monitoring the receipt, manufacture, distribution and disposition of drug precursors in its' operation

16.19.22.8

PERMISSIBLE ACTIVITIES:

- Pharmacy technician activities under the direct supervision of a pharmacist shall be limited to tasks enumerated in policies and procedures implemented by the pharmacist-in-charge that do not require professional judgment.

16.19.22.9

TRAINING AND EDUCATION:

- The pharmacist-in-charge shall ensure that the pharmacy technician has completed initial training which includes:
    o federal and state laws and regulations that affect pharmacy practice; specific regulations which address the use of supportive personnel and technicians;
    o ethical and professional standards of practice;
    o medical and pharmaceutical terminology, symbols and abbreviations used in the practice of pharmacy and components of a prescription;
    o pharmaceutical calculations necessary for the preparation and dispensing of drug products;
    o manufacturing, preparation, packaging, labeling and proper storage of drug products;
    o dosage forms and routes of administration; And

- o trade and generic names for medications frequently dispensed by the pharmacy;

- o basic comprehension of pharmacology;

- o basic knowledge of appropriate pharmacy references.

- If the duties of the technician will include the preparation of sterile products then, in addition to the training and education requirements listed in this section, the technician will complete training outlined in Subsection C of 16.19.36.13 NMAC.

- A written record of training and education will be maintained by the pharmacy technician and contain the following:

  - o name of person receiving the training;

  - o date(s) of the training;

  - o description of the topics covered;

  - o names of the person(s) who provided the training; and

  - o signature of the technician and the technician training sponsor.

- A written record of training and education must be submitted to the board with certification exam documentation to obtain certified pharmacy technician registration.

- All technicians are required to obtain board approved certification within one year of registration with the board as a technician. Extensions will no longer be granted to pharmacy technicians registered on or after November 15, 2010.

- The pharmacist-in-charge shall be responsible for the implementation of policies and procedures for additional training appropriate to duties and responsibilities performed by a pharmacy technician as well as an ongoing quality assurance plan to assure competency.

16.19.22.10

RATIO OF TECHNICIANS TO PHARMACISTS:

- The permissible ratio of pharmacy technicians to pharmacists on duty is to be determined by the pharmacist in charge.

- The board reserves the right to impose a ratio of pharmacy technicians to pharmacists if circumstances so dictate.

16.19.22.11

IMPROPER ACTIVITIES OF PHARMACY TECHNICIANS:

- The supervising pharmacist and the pharmacist-in-charge are responsible for the actions of pharmacy technicians. Performance of tasks by the pharmacy technician and support personnel outside the limits of the regulations that are authorized by the supervising pharmacist shall constitute unprofessional conduct on the part of the pharmacist and the pharmacist-in-charge.

- The following responsibilities require the use of professional judgment and therefore shall be performed only by a pharmacist or pharmacist intern:

    - receipt of all new verbal prescription orders and reduction to writing;

    - evaluation and interpretation of the prescription order and any necessary clinical clarification prior to dispensing;

    - clinical consultation with a patient or his agent regarding a prescription or over-the-counter drug;

    - evaluation of available clinical data in patient medication record system;

- oral communication with the patient or patient's agent of information, as defined in the section under patient counseling, in order to improve therapy by ensuring proper use of drugs and devices;

- professional consultation with the prescriber, the prescriber's agent, or any other health care professional or authorized agent regarding a patient and any medical information pertaining to the prescription.

ONLY A PHARMACIST SHALL PERFORM THE FOLLOWING DUTIES:

- final check on all aspects of the completed prescription including sterile products and cytotoxic preparations, and assumption of the responsibility for the filled prescription, including, but not limited to, appropriateness of dose, accuracy of drug, strength, labeling, verification of ingredients and proper container;

- evaluation of pharmaceuticals for formulary selection within the facility;

- supervision of all pharmacy technicians and support personnel activities including preparations, mixing, assembling, packaging, labeling and storage of medication;

- ensure the pharmacy technicians and support personnel have been properly trained for the duties they may perform;

- any verbal communication with a patient or patient's representative regarding a change in drug therapy or performing therapeutic interchanges (i.e. drugs with similar effects in specific therapeutic categories); this does not apply to substitution of generic equivalents;

- any other duty required of a pharmacist by any federal or state law.

- In accordance with Section 61-11-20 NMSA 1978 a pharmacy technicians registration may be revoked, denied, or suspended for grounds stated in Subsection A of Section 61-11-20 NMSA 1978.

16.19.22.14

REGISTRATION OF PHARMACY TECHNICIANS:

- Application (and required registration fee) shall be submitted to the board prior to performing any technician duties. Non-certified pharmacy technicians must:

  o Complete requirements for certified pharmacy technician within one year of original application.

  o Not re-apply with the board of pharmacy as a non-certified pharmacy technician unless enrolled in a board recognized technician training program.

  o Provide the name of the technician training sponsor responsible for training and education with application.

  o Provide documentation of training and completion of certification exam to be registered as a certified pharmacy technician.

- Registration for certified pharmacy technicians will expire biennially on the last day of their birth month and must be renewed prior to expiration. Registration renewal applications must include documentation of current national certification.

16.19.22.15

CHANGE OF ADDRESS:

- Pharmacy technicians shall report in writing or through the online process available on the board's website of any change of address or employment to the board within 10 days.

16.19.22.16

PHARMACY TECHNICIAN ADMINISTRATION OF VACCINES:

- A certified pharmacy technician may administer vaccines prescribed by and under the direct supervision of a New Mexico licensed pharmacist with current immunization prescriptive authority "qualified pharmacist," if all requirements of this section are met.

- Training and education:

- The pharmacy technician must successfully complete an accreditation council for pharmacy education (ACPE) accredited immunization certification course for pharmacy technicians. This training must include study materials, hands-on injection technique, and the recognition and treatment of emergency reactions to vaccines. Pharmacy technicians who successfully completed said training prior to the enactment date of this section will be grandfathered.

- The pharmacy technician must complete and maintain current basic life support/cardiopulmonary resuscitation (BLS/CPR) certification.

- Continuing Education: Any pharmacy technician engaging in administration of vaccines shall complete a minimum of 0.2 CEU of ACPE accredited vaccine related continuing education during each registration period.

- Competency assurance:

- o The pharmacist-in-charge is responsible for ensuring that the technician has completed the required training; and possesses the knowledge, skills and abilities to appropriately engage in vaccine administration.

- o The pharmacist-in-charge is responsible for developing, implementing and maintaining proper policies and procedures, which must include training and competency oversight to ensure compliance with the requirements of this section. Such procedures shall include an initial observation by a qualified pharmacist to ensure proper administration technique.

- o The pharmacist-in-charge and technician are responsible for maintaining training and education documentation.

- Oversight and activities:

  - o While the pharmacy technician may draw up the vaccine into a syringe, the supervising qualified pharmacist is responsible for final verification.

  - o The qualified pharmacist must provide patient counseling, as appropriate.

  - o The identity of the pharmacy technician who administered each dose of vaccine will be documented. The qualified pharmacist is responsible for ensuring proper documentation.

  - o Supervision: A qualified pharmacist may not supervise more than two pharmacy technicians administering vaccines in a pharmacy setting. A pharmacist whose duties are dedicated to vaccination (e.g. vaccination clinic) may not supervise more than six qualified pharmacy technicians administering vaccines at one time. It is the responsibility of the pharmacist in charge to ensure adequate staffing levels for duties performed.

- All records required under this section shall be readily available for inspection and produced to the board or the board's agent upon request.

16.19.24.10

CONSULTANT PHARMACIST:

- Any EMS licensed by the Board is required to have a consultant pharmacist as defined in 16 NMAC 19.4.11. In addition, the consultant pharmacist shall:

- review all instances in which controlled substances were used, and review all or a sample of instances in which other drugs were used, at least every 90 days;

- report in writing any exceptions to the Medical Director and the chief executive within 24 hours upon learning of same;

- otherwise make a written report to the Medical Director and chief executive at least annually on the EMS's drug handling practices, including corrective action taken on exception; and

- such reports shall be available for review by the Board upon request.

- the consultant pharmacist will develop policies and procedures for EMS regarding the following:

- functions of consultant pharmacist;

- formulary;

- security of drugs;

- equipment;

- universal precautions;

- licensing;

- drug storage;

- packaging and repackaging;

- distribution records;

- document use of expired drugs for training;

- administration and/or patient care records;

- storage of drugs in jump kits;

- drug destruction and records;

- drug and device procurement;

- receipt of drugs and devices;

- delivery of drugs and devices;

- designate items to be included in jump kits, define par levels of drugs, storage conditions and locations where the jump kits are in use.

16.19.24.11

STORAGE OF DANGEROUS DRUGS BY EMS:

- All dangerous drugs must be stored with appropriate security to limit access when authorized personnel are not present. Extra precautions shall be provided for security of controlled substances.

- Jump kits shall be kept in the possession of a licensed emergency practitioner or in a locked compartment of a mobile unit when not in use.

- Jump kits shall be stored in the facility if the mobile unit is parked outside of a secure vehicle bay.

- Drugs shall be stored in an area: providing proper ventilation, lighting, and temperature controls as specified by the drug manufacturer.

- Drugs that are outdated or which have been exposed to adverse conditions shall be segregated from the inventory and held for disposition by the consultant pharmacist.

16.19.24.12

Administration of dangerous drugs by EMS:

- EMS drug administration shall be limited to drugs currently authorized by scopes of practice for EMS personnel. Each licensee shall provide a formulary to the Board on an annual basis or as changes occur.

- EMS shall keep an up to date record in readily retrievable format for review by the Board, indicating the following information for the administration of all dangerous drugs;
  - date of administration;
  - name of patient;
  - drug name and dosage administered;
  - name of physician responsible for the order, if by other than the Medical Director's protocols;
  - name of EMS personnel administering the drug or drugs.

- EMS shall keep SCHEDULE II controlled substances administration and receipt records separately from other drug records.

- EMS may keep SCHEDULE III - V controlled substances receipt and administration records in the same record in which dangerous drugs are recorded, provided a mechanism is employed to identify these records (such as a red "C" marked in the margin of these entries).

- All drug receipt and administration records must be readily retrievable and retained for a period of at least three years.

16.19.25

THE PHARMACIST IN CHARGE SHALL:

- Develop and implement written error prevention procedures as part of the Policy and Procedures Manual.

- Report incidents, including relevant status updates, to the Board on Board approved forms within fifteen (15) days of discovery.

16.19.25.9

THE BOARD SHALL:

- Maintain confidentiality of information relating to the reporter and the patient identifiers.

- Compile and publish, in the newsletter and on the Board web site, report information and prevention recommendations.

- Assure reports are used in a constructive and non-punitive manner.

16.19.26.8

REFERRAL:

Any pharmacist not certified to provide a prescriptive authority service is required to refer patients to a pharmacist or other provider who provides such a service.

16.19.26.9

VACCINES:

- Protocol:

- Prescriptive authority for vaccines shall be exercised solely in accordance with the written protocol for vaccine prescriptive authority approved by the board.

- Any pharmacist exercising prescriptive authority for vaccines must maintain a current copy of the protocol for vaccine prescriptive authority approved by the board.

- Education and training:

- The pharmacist must successfully complete a course of training, accredited by the accreditation council for pharmacy education (ACPE), provided by:
  - the centers for disease control and prevention (CDC); or
  - a similar health authority or professional body approved by the board.
  - Training must include study materials, hands-on training and techniques for administering vaccines, comply with current CDC guidelines, and provide instruction and experiential training in the following content areas:
  - mechanisms of action for vaccines, contraindication, drug interaction, and monitoring after vaccine administration.
  - standards for pediatric, adolescent, and adult immunization practices.
  - basic immunology and vaccine protection.
  - vaccine-preventable diseases.
  - recommended pediatric, adolescent, and adult immunization schedule.
  - vaccine storage management.
  - biohazard waste disposal and sterile techniques.

- o informed consent.

- o physiology and techniques for vaccine administration.

- o pre- and post-vaccine assessment and counseling.

- o immunization record management.

- o management of adverse events, including identification, appropriate response, documentation, and reporting.

- reimbursement procedures and vaccine coverage by federal, state and local entities.

- Continuing education: Any pharmacist exercising prescriptive authority for vaccines shall complete a minimum of 0.2 CEU of live ACPE approved vaccine related continuing education every two years. Such continuing education shall be in addition to requirements in 16.19.4.10 NMAC.

- Basic life support/cardiopulmonary resuscitation (BLS/CPR): Any pharmacist exercising prescriptive authority for vaccines shall complete and have current live BLS/CPR certification.

- Authorized drugs:

- Prescriptive authority shall be limited to those drugs and vaccines delineated in the written protocol for vaccine prescriptive authority approved by the board, and.

- Other vaccines as determined by the CDC, the advisory committee on immunization practices (ACIP) or New Mexico department of health that may be required to protect the public health and safety

- Records:

- The prescribing pharmacist must generate a written or electronic prescription for any dangerous drug authorized.

- Informed consent must be documented in accordance with the written protocol for vaccine prescriptive authority approved by the board and a record of such consent maintained in the pharmacy for a period of at least three years.

- Notification: Upon signed consent of the patient or guardian the pharmacist shall update the New Mexico department of health immunization program's electronic database (NMSIIS) of any vaccine administered.

16.19.26.12

NALOXONE FOR OPIOID OVERDOSE:

- Protocol:

- Prescriptive authority for naloxone drug therapy shall be exercised solely in accordance with the written protocol for naloxone drug therapy approved by the board.

- Any pharmacist exercising prescriptive authority for naloxone drug therapy must maintain a current copy of the written protocol for naloxone drug therapy approved by the board.

- Education and training:

- The pharmacist must successfully complete a course of training, accredited by the accreditation council for pharmacy education (ACPE), in the subject area of naloxone for opioid overdose drug therapy provided by:
  - o the New Mexico pharmacist's association; or
  - o a similar health authority or professional body approved by the board.

- Training must include study materials and instruction in the following content areas:
  - o mechanisms of action.
  - o contraindications.

- identifying indications for the use of naloxone drug therapy.

- patient screening criteria.

- counseling and training patient and caregiver regarding the safety, efficacy and potential adverse effects of naloxone.

- evaluating patient's medical profile for drug interactions.

- referring patient for follow-up care with primary healthcare provider.

- informed consent.

- record management.

- management of adverse events.

- Continuing education: Any pharmacist exercising prescriptive authority for naloxone drug therapy shall complete a minimum of 0.2 CEU of live ACPE approved naloxone drug therapy related continuing education every two years. Such continuing education shall be in addition to requirements in 16.19.4.10 NMAC.

- Authorized drug(s):

- Prescriptive authority shall be limited to naloxone and shall include any device(s) approved for the administration of naloxone.

- Prescriptive authority for naloxone drug therapy shall be limited to naloxone as delineated in the written protocol for naloxone drug therapy approved by the board.

- Records:

- The prescribing pharmacist must generate a written or electronic prescription for any naloxone dispensed.

- Informed consent must be documented in accordance with the approved protocol for naloxone drug therapy and a record of such consent maintained in the pharmacy for a period of at least three years.

- Notification: Upon signed consent of the patient, the pharmacist shall notify the patient's designated physician or primary care provider within 15 days of naloxone dispensing.

16.19.26.13

HORMONAL CONTRACEPTION DRUG THERAPY:

- Protocol:

- Prescriptive authority for hormonal contraception drug therapy shall be exercised solely in accordance with the written protocol for hormonal contraception drug therapy approved by the board.

- Any pharmacist exercising prescriptive authority for hormonal contraception drug therapy must maintain a current copy of the written protocol for hormonal contraception drug therapy approved by the board.

- Education and training:

- The pharmacist must successfully complete a course of training, accredited by the accreditation council for pharmacy education (ACPE), in the subject of hormonal contraception drug therapy provided by:
  - o the New Mexico pharmacist's association or;
  - o a similar health authority or professional body approved by the board.

- Training must include study materials and instruction in the following content areas:
  - o mechanisms of action, contraindication, drug interaction and monitoring of hormonal contraception drug therapy.
  - o current standards for prescribing hormonal contraception drug therapy.
  - o identifying indications for use of hormonal contraception drug therapy.

- o interviewing patient to establish need for hormonal contraception drug therapy.

- o counseling patient regarding the safety, efficacy and potential adverse effects of drug products for hormonal contraception.

- o evaluating patient's medical profile for drug interaction.

- o referring patient follow-up care with primary healthcare provider.

- o informed consent.

- o management of adverse events, including identification, appropriate response, documentation and reporting.

- Continuing education: any pharmacist exercising prescriptive authority for hormonal contraception drug therapy shall complete a minimum of 0.2 CEU of live ACPE approved hormonal contraception drug therapy related continuing education every two years. Such continuing education shall be in addition to requirements in 16.19.4.10 NMAC.

- Authorized drugs:

- Prescriptive authority shall be limited to hormonal contraception drug therapy and shall exclude any device intended to prevent pregnancy after intercourse.

- Prescriptive authority for hormonal contraception drug therapy shall be limited to those drugs delineated in the written protocol for hormonal contraception drug therapy approved by the board.

- Records:

- The prescribing pharmacist must generate a written or electronic prescription for any dangerous drug authorized.

- Informed consent must be documented in accordance with the approved protocol for hormonal contraception drug therapy and a record of such consent maintained in the pharmacy for a period of at least three years.

- Notification: Upon signed consent of the patient or guardian, the pharmacist shall notify the patient's designated physician or primary care provider of hormonal contraception drug therapy prescribed.

16.19.28.8

REGISTRATION:

- A person who is not a licensed optometrist or a licensed physician shall not sell or dispense a contact lens to a resident of this state unless he is registered with the board of pharmacy.

- Pharmacies, hospitals and clinics licensed by the board are exempt from this regulation.

- Registration will be submitted in forms provided by the board with the appropriate fee attached as a check or money order.

- Fees for registration are listed in 16.19.12 NMAC.

- Period of registration is for two years with renewals due by the last day of the expiration month listed on the registration.

16.19.28.9

POLICY MANUAL:

- A policy manual containing at a minimum the information listed below shall be submitted with the registration application. The initial manual, must be approved by the board and any subsequent changes or modifications require prior approval of the board or its agent.

- A contact lens may not be sold, dispensed, or distributed to a patient in this state by a seller of contact lenses unless one of the following has occurred:

- o the patient has given or mailed the seller an original, valid, unexpired written contact lens prescription.

- o the prescribing licensed optometrist has given, mailed or transmitted by facsimile transmission a copy of a valid, unexpired written contact lens prescription to a seller designated in writing by the patient to act on the patient's behalf; or

- o the prescribing licensed optometrist has orally or in writing verified the valid, unexpired prescription to a seller designated by the patient to act on his behalf.

- The prescription contains all the information necessary for the replacement contact lens prescription to be properly dispensed, including the:

  - o lens manufacturer.

  - o type of lens.

  - o power of the lens.

  - o base curve.

  - o lens size.

  - o name of the patient.

  - o date the prescription was given to the patient.

  - o name and office location of the licensed optometrist who writes the replacement contact lens prescription; and

  - o expiration date of the replacement contact lens prescription.

- A person other than a licensed optometrist or physician who fills a contact lens prescription shall maintain a record of that prescription for three years.

- Security requirements: restricting access, to all lenses and patient health records, to authorized personnel only.

- Storage requirements: The registrant must have policies and procedures for maintaining the proper storage conditions for contact lenses. The lenses must be stored at the licensed location.

16.19.29.8

MANDATORY REPORTING OF PRESCRIPTION INFORMATION TO THE PMP:

- The board shall monitor the dispensing of all schedule II - V controlled substances by all dispensers licensed to dispense such substances to patients in this state.

- Each dispenser shall submit to the board by electronic means information regarding each prescription dispensed for a drug included under Subsection A of this section. Information to be submitted for each prescription as well as the standards for how this information shall be formatted, not contrary to law, is defined in the PMP data reporting manual available on the state PMP website at http://nmpmp.org shall include at a minimum:

  o dispenser NPI number.

  o dispenser NCPDP number.

  o dispenser DEA number.

  o patient name.

  o patient address.

  o patient date of birth.

  o patient gender.

  o reporting status (new, revised, void).

  o prescription number.

- o date prescription written.

- o refills authorized.

- o date prescription filled.

- o refill number.

- o product ID (NDC) + product ID qualifier.

- o quantity dispensed.

- o days' supply.

- o drug dosage units.

- o transmission form of Rx origin.

- o payment type.

- o prescriber NPI number; (except veterinarians)

- o prescriber DEA number.

- Dispenser reporting:

  - o each dispenser shall submit the information required under Subsection B of this section in accordance with transmission methods and frequency established by the board; but shall report within one business day of the prescription being filled.

  - o if a dispenser pharmacy did not dispense any schedule II – V controlled substances during an operating business day, the dispenser shall submit a "zero report" within one business day. Information to be submitted with each zero report as well as the standards for how this information shall be formatted, not contrary to law, is defined in the PMP data reporting manual available on the state PMP website at http://nmpmp.org shall include at a minimum:

    - ▪ dispenser DEA number.

- reporting start date; and

- reporting end date.

  o the PMP director shall have the authority to approve submission schedules that exceed one business day.

- Corrections to information submitted to the PMP must be addressed including:

  o file upload or "outstanding uncorrected errors" as defined in the PMP data reporting manual.

  o prescriptions that were not dispensed to the patient must be voided from the PMP.

  o incorrect information in prescriptions records submitted to the PMP must be submitted to the PMP database within five business days once the dispenser has been notified or becomes aware of the incorrect information.

16.19.29.9

DISCLOSURE OF PRESCRIPTION INFORMATION:

- Prescription information submitted to the board shall not be subject to the Inspection of the Public Records Act, Sections 14-2-1 through 14-2-12 NMSA 1978 and shall be confidential except as provided in Subsections C through G of 16.19.29.9 NMAC.

- The board shall maintain procedures to ensure that the privacy and confidentiality of patients and patient information collected, recorded, transmitted, and maintained in the PMP is not disclosed to persons except as provided in Subsection C through G of 16.19.29.9 NMAC.

- Board inspectors may review prescription information after receiving complaints, and in the course of their enforcement of board administered statutes and regulations.

- The board shall be authorized to provide PMP information to the following persons:
    o persons authorized to prescribe or dispense controlled substances, for the purpose of providing medical or pharmaceutical care for their patients.

    o a consultant pharmacist for the purpose of providing pharmaceutical care for a facility's patients; and in ensuring that facility records appropriately account for controlled substance receipt, administration and disposition.

    o a delegate designated by a practitioner; or pharmacist; who must also maintain an active account, can designate one or more (up to four) delegates for the purpose of requesting and receiving PMP reports for the practitioner or pharmacist; the practitioner or pharmacist shall be responsible for terminating the delegate's access to the PMP within five business days of a delegate's authorization ending.

    o state practitioner licensing boards whose licensees have prescriptive authority for controlled substances, including the medical board, board of nursing, board of veterinarian medicine, board of dental health care, board of examiners in optometry, board of osteopathic medicine, board of acupuncture and oriental medicine, and board of podiatry, as the PMP information relates to their licensees.

    o practitioner licensing authorities of other states if their licensees practice in this state or prescriptions provided by their licensees are dispensed in this state.

    o local, state and federal law enforcement or prosecutorial officials engaged in an ongoing investigation of an individual in the enforcement of the laws governing licit drugs.

    o the state human services department regarding Medicaid program recipients.

    o a state metropolitan, magistrate and district, or federal court as required by a grand jury subpoena or criminal court order.

- state drug court personnel as authorized by the PMP director.

- personnel of the board for purposes of administration and enforcement of this rule or of 16.19.20 NMAC.

- the prescription monitoring program of another state or group of states with whom the state has established an interoperability agreement.

- a living individual who request's his or her own PMP report in accordance with procedures established under the Pharmacy Act, Subsection D of Section 61-11-2 NMSA 1978 and Subsection H of 16.19.6.23 NMAC, or an agent authorized by the living individual along with a valid HIPAA release form or court issued subpoena, or.

- a parent to have access to the prescription records about his or her minor child, as his or her minor child's personal representative when such access is not inconsistent with state or other laws.

- licensed healthcare professionals (nurses, pharmacists and practitioners) from Medicare, health insurers, workers compensation program/insurers and pharmacy benefit managers for persons enrolled in or covered by their programs, as part of patient care for those persons.

- The board shall use de-identified data obtained from the PMP database to identify and report to state and local public health authorities the geographic areas of the state where anomalous prescribing dispensing or use of controlled substances is occurring.

- The board shall share PMP database data with the department of health for the purpose of tracking inappropriate prescribing and misuse of controlled substances, including drug overdose.

- The board shall provide data to public or private entities for statistical, research, or educational purposes after removing information that could be used to identify individual patients and persons who have received prescriptions from dispensers.

- PMP information gained from other states' prescription monitoring programs shall not be subject to civil subpoena, nor shall such information be disclosed, discoverable, or compelled to be produced in any civil proceeding, nor shall such records be deemed admissible as evidence in any civil proceeding for any reason.

16.19.29.10

DISCLOSURE OF AUDIT TRAIL INFORMATION:

- Audit trail information maintained by the board shall not be subject to the Inspection of Public Records Act, Sections 14-2-1 through 14-2-12 NMSA 1978, and shall be confidential except as provided in Subsection C and D of 16.19.29.10 NMAC.

- The board shall maintain procedures to ensure that the privacy and confidentiality of patients and patient information collected, recorded, transmitted, and maintained in the PMP is not disclosed to persons except as provided in Subsection C and D of 16.19.29.10 NMAC.

- Board inspectors may review audit trail information after receiving complaints, and in the course of their enforcement of board administered statutes and regulations.

- The board shall be authorized to provide audit trail information to the following persons:
  - state practitioner licensing boards whose licensees have prescriptive authority for controlled substances, including the medical board, board of nursing, board of veterinary medicine, board of dental health care, board of optometry, board of

osteopathic medicine, board of acupuncture and oriental medicine, and board of podiatry, as the audit trail information relates to their licensees for the purposes of reviewing compliance with PMP utilization.

- o practitioner licensing authorities of other states if their licensees practice in this state or prescriptions provided by their licensees are dispensed in this state as the audit trail information relates to their licensees for the purposes of reviewing compliance with PMP utilization requirements.

- o personnel of the board for purposes of administration and enforcement of this rule or of 16.19.20 NMAC.

- o the board shall share PMP database data with the department of health for the purpose of tracking inappropriate prescribing and misuse of controlled substances, including drug overdose.

- Audit trail information shall not be subject to civil subpoena, nor shall such information be disclosed, discoverable, or compelled to be produced in any civil proceeding, nor shall such records be deemed admissible as evidence in any civil proceeding for any reason.

16.19.29.11

AUTHORITY TO CONTRACT:

- The board may contract with another agency of this state or with a private vendor, as necessary, to ensure the effective operation of the PMP. A contractor shall comply with the provisions regarding confidentiality of prescription information in 16.19.29.9 NMAC and shall be subject to the penalties specified in 16.19.29.14 NMAC.

16.19.29.12

REGISTRATION FOR ACCESS TO PRESCRIPTION INFORMATION:

- Persons authorized for access to PMP information as listed in Paragraphs (1) through (10) and (14) of Subsection D of 16.19.29.9 NMAC must apply for access as described at the PMP website located at http://nmpmp.org or as otherwise indicated. Persons granted access must maintain individual accounts and shall not share access information with other persons.

- All persons authorized for access to PMP information and applying for such access to the PMP shall successfully complete a web-based training program as determined by the PMP director.

- Persons reporting prescription information to the PMP, but not authorized for access to PMP information must also apply for access as described at the PMP website located at http://nmpmp.org or as otherwise indicated.

- The PMP director shall have the authority to set account access and registration renewal requirements necessary for accounts to be considered active and shall also have authority to cancel inactive accounts.

16.19.29.13

INFORMATION EXCHANGE WITH OTHER PRESCRIPTION MONITORING PROGRAMS:

- The board may provide PMP information to other states' prescription monitoring programs and such information may be used by those programs consistent with the provisions of this rule.

- The board may request and receive PMP information from other states' prescription monitoring programs and may use such information under provisions of this rule.

- The board may develop the capability to transmit information to and receive information from other prescription monitoring programs employing the standards of interoperability.

- The board may enter into written agreements with other states' prescription monitoring programs or other persons hosting compatible information sharing technologies for the purpose of describing the terms and conditions for sharing of PMP information under this section.

16.19.29.14

PENALTIES:

- A dispenser who knowingly fails to submit prescription monitoring information to the board as required by this rule or knowingly submits incorrect prescription information shall be subject to disciplinary proceedings as defined in Section 61-11-20 of the Pharmacy Act NMSA 1978.

- Prescription information submitted to the PMP is protected health information. Persons with access to the PMP shall exercise due diligence in protecting this information and access it only as necessary in the course of legitimate professional regulatory, or law enforcement duties.

- A person found to be in violation of this section may be subject to one or more of the following actions.
    - Termination of access to PMP information.
    - A complaint may be filed with his or her appropriate professional licensing entities.

16.19.30.8

PERSONNEL:

- Pharmacist-in-charge. The pharmacist-in-charge shall have the responsibility for, at a minimum, the following concerning non-sterile compounding:
    - determining that all personnel involved in non-sterile compounding possess the education, training, and proficiency necessary to properly and safely perform compounding duties undertaken or supervised.
    - determining that all personnel involved in non-sterile compounding obtain continuing education appropriate for the type of compounding done by the personnel.
    - assuring that the equipment used in compounding is properly maintained.
    - maintaining an appropriate environment in the area where non-sterile compounding occurs.
    - assuring that effective quality control procedures are developed and followed; and

- assuring availability of current reference source for the type of compounding conducted.

- Pharmacists. Special requirements for non-sterile compounding.
  - all pharmacists engaged in compounding shall:
    - possess the education, training, and proficiency necessary to properly and safely perform compounding duties undertaken or supervised and
    - obtain continuing education for the type of compounding done by the pharmacist.
  - A pharmacist shall inspect and approve all components, drug product containers, closures, labeling and any other material involved in the compounding process.
  - A pharmacist shall review all compounding records for accuracy and conduct in-process and final checks to assure that errors have not occurred in the compounding process.
  - A pharmacist is responsible for the proper maintenance, cleanliness and use of all equipment used in the compounding process.

- Pharmacy technicians. All technicians engaged in compounding shall:
  - possess the education, training and proficiency necessary to properly and safely perform compounding duties undertaken.
  - obtain continuing education for the type of compounding done by the pharmacy technician; and
  - perform compounding duties under the direct supervision of and responsible to a pharmacist.

- Training. All personnel involved in non-sterile compounding shall be trained and must participate in continuing relevant training programs.

16.19.30.9

OPERATIONAL STANDARDS:

- General requirements.

    o Non-sterile drug products may be compounded in licensed pharmacies as a result of a practitioner's prescription order based on the practitioner-patient-pharmacist relationship in the course of professional practice.

    o Preparing limited quantities of prescription drug orders in anticipation based upon a history of receiving valid prescriptions issued within an established practitioner-patient-pharmacist relationship in the course of professional practice.

        ▪ The beyond-use date should be based on the criteria outlined in USP Chapter <795>.

        ▪ Any product compounded in anticipation of future prescription drug or medication orders shall be labeled. Each label shall contain:

        ▪ name and strength of the compounded medication or list of the active ingredient and strengths.

        ▪ facility's lot number.

        ▪ beyond-use date.

        ▪ quantity or amount in the container.

- Commercially available product may be compounded for dispensing to individual patients provided the following conditions are met:

        ▪ the commercial product is not reasonably available from normal distribution channels in a timely manner to meet patient's needs; and the prescribing practitioner has requested that the drug be compounded; or

- if the compounded product is changed to produce for that patient a significant difference, as authorized by the prescriber, between the compounded drug and the comparable commercially available drug product, or if use of the compounded product is in the best interest of the patient; "significant difference" would include the removal of a dye for medical reason such as an allergic reaction; when a compounded product is to be dispensed in place of a commercially available product, the prescriber and patient shall be informed that the product will be compounded.

- Compounding veterinary preparations.

- Preparations for animals may be compounded based on an order or prescription from a duly authorized veterinarian.

- These preparations are to be handled and filled the same as the human prescriptions.

- Compounding of drugs for animals must be in accordance with the Animal Medicinal Drug Use Clarification Act of 1994 or successor Act.

- A licensed pharmacy may compound veterinary drug preparations in reasonable quantities, in accordance with Paragraph (5) of Subsection DDD of 16.19.8.7 NMAC to be used by veterinarians in their office for administration to patients ("office use preparations").

- Compounded office use preparations may be dispensed by a veterinarian to clients only under the following conditions:
  - a valid veterinarian client patient relationship exists.
  - the patient has an emergency condition that the compounded drug is necessary to treat.

- dispensed amount is for use in a single course of treatment, not to exceed a 120-hour supply.

    o timely access to a compounding pharmacy is not available; and

    o the medication is not a controlled substance.

    o Compounded controlled substance veterinary office use preparations may be distributed by a pharmacy under the following conditions:

    o the preparation is not readily available from an outsourcing facility.

    o ordering and distribution occur in compliance with applicable state and federal law.

    o the pharmacy shall be registered with the DEA as a manufacturer; and

    o in addition to other required labeling, such preparations shall bear a statement "For administration only. Not for dispensing or resale."

- Prohibition on wholesaling:

- Office use preparations will not be distributed by a person other than the pharmacy that compounded such veterinary drug preparations.

- This does not prohibit administration or dispensing pursuant to a prescription drug order executed in accordance with federal and state law; and the conditions of this Paragraph (4).

- Providing samples of compounded veterinary preparations is prohibited.

- Compounding pharmacies/pharmacists may advertise and promote the fact that they provide non-sterile prescription compounding services which may include specific drug products and classes of drugs.

- Environment.

- Pharmacies regularly engaging in compounding shall have a designated and adequate area for the safe and orderly compounding of drug products including the placement of equipment and materials. Pharmacies involved in occasional compounding shall prepare an area prior to each compounding activity, which is adequate for safe and orderly compounding.

- Only personnel authorized by the responsible pharmacist shall be in the immediate vicinity of a drug compounding operation.

- A sink with hot and cold running water, exclusive of rest room facilities, shall be accessible to the compounding areas and be maintained in a sanitary condition.

- When drug products that require special precautions to prevent contamination, such as penicillin, are involved in a compounding operation, appropriate measures, including dedication of equipment for such operations or the meticulous cleaning of contaminated equipment prior to its' use for the preparation of other drug products, must be used in order to prevent cross-contamination.

- Equipment and supplies. The pharmacy shall:

- have a Class A prescription balance, or analytical balance and weights, when necessary, which shall be properly maintained and subject to inspection by the New Mexico board of pharmacy; and

- have equipment and utensils necessary for the proper compounding of prescription or medication drug orders; such equipment and utensils used in the compounding process shall be:

    o of appropriate design and capacity and be operated within designated operational limits.

    o of suitable composition so that surfaces that contact components, in-process material or drug products shall not be reactive, additive, or absorptive so as to alter the safety, identity, strength, quality or purity of the drug product beyond the desired result.

- o cleaned and sanitized appropriately prior to each use; and

- o routinely inspected, calibrated when necessary or checked to ensure proper performance.

- Labeling. In addition to the labeling requirements of the pharmacy's specific license classification, the label dispensed or distributed pursuant to a prescription or medication drug order shall contain the following:

  - o the generic name(s) or the designated name and the strength of the compounded preparation.

  - o the quantity dispensed.

  - o the date on which the product was compounded.

  - o a lot or batch number; and

  - o the beyond-use date after which the compounded preparation should not be used.

  - o in the absence of stability information applicable for a specific drug or preparation in the USP/NF the preparation shall adhere to the following maximum beyond-use date guidelines:

  - o for non-aqueous formulations - the BUD is not later than the time remaining until the earliest expiration date of any API or six months, whichever is earlier.

  - o for water-containing oral formulations - the BUD is not later than 14 days when stored at controlled cold temperatures.

  - o for water-containing topical/dermal and mucosal liquid and semisolid formulations - the BUD is not later than 30 days.

  - o beyond-use date limits may be exceeded when supported by valid scientific stability information for the specific compounded preparation; the BUD shall not be later than the expiration date on the container of any component.

- Drugs, components and material used in non-sterile compounding.

- Drugs used in non-sterile compounding shall preferably be a USP/NF grade substance manufactured in a FDA registered facility.

- In the event that USP/NF grade substances are not available, documentation of stability and purity must be established and documented.

- A pharmacy may not compound a drug product which has been withdrawn or removed from the market for safety reasons.

- Compounding process. The safety, quality and performance of compounded prescriptions depend on correct ingredients and calculations, accurate and precise measurements, appropriate formulation conditions and procedures, and prudent pharmaceutical judgment. Each pharmacy shall develop and follow written SOP's based on established compounding procedures as outlined in chapter 795 of the USP/NF concerning pharmacy compounding of non-sterile preparations designed to ensure accountability, accuracy, quality, safety, and uniformity in the compounding process.

- Quality control.

- The safety, quality, and monitoring is used to insure that the output of compounded drug products for uniformity and consistency such as capsule weight variations, adequacy of mixing, clarity or pH of solutions are met. When developing these procedures, pharmacy personnel shall consider the provisions of Chapter 795 of the USP/NF concerning pharmacy compounding of non-sterile preparations, chapter 1075 of the USP/NF concerning good compounding practices, and chapter 1160 of the USP/NF concerning pharmaceutical calculations in prescription compounding. Such procedures shall be documented and be available for inspection.

- Compounding procedures that are routinely performed, including batch compounding, shall be completed and verified according to written procedures. The act of verification of a compounding procedure involves checking to ensure that calculations, weighing and measuring, order of mixing, and compounding techniques were appropriate and accurately performed.

- Unless otherwise indicated or appropriate, compounded preparations are to be prepared to ensure that each preparation shall contain not less than 90.0 percent and not more than 110.0 percent of the theoretically calculated and labeled quantity of active ingredient per unit volume and not less than 90.0 percent and not more than 110.0 percent of the theoretically calculated weight or volume per unit of the preparation.

16.19.31.8

EMERGENCY TEMPORARY PHARMACIST LICENSE:

- Emergency temporary pharmacist license. In an emergency situation, the board may grant a pharmacist who holds a license to practice pharmacy in another state an emergency temporary pharmacist license to practice in New Mexico. The following is applicable for the emergency temporary pharmacist license.

- An applicant for an emergency temporary pharmacist license under this section must:
  o hold a current pharmacist license in another state and that license and other licenses held by the applicant in any other state may not be suspended, revoked, canceled, surrendered, or otherwise restricted for any reason; and
  o be sponsored by a pharmacy with an active license in New Mexico.

- To qualify for an emergency temporary pharmacist license, the applicant must submit an application including the following information:
  - name, address, and phone number of the applicant.
  - name and license number of the pharmacist-in-charge of the sponsoring pharmacy.
  - name and license number of the sponsoring pharmacy; and
  - any other information that is required by the board.
- An emergency temporary pharmacist license shall be valid for a period as determined by the executive director of the board not to exceed six months. The executive director, in his/her discretion, may renew the license for an additional six months, if the emergency situation still exists.
- The board will notify the sponsoring pharmacy of the approval of an emergency temporary pharmacist license.
- Limitations on practice. A holder of an emergency temporary pharmacist license:
  - may only practice in the sponsoring pharmacy; and
  - must notify the board in writing, prior to beginning employment in another sponsoring pharmacy.

16.19.31.9

PROVISIONS FOR PHARMACIST LICENSURE DURING DECLARED DISASTER:

- Emergency provisions for license by endorsement. Pharmacist currently licensed in a state in which a federal disaster has been declared may be licensed by endorsement in New

Mexico during the four months following the declared disaster at no cost with the following requirements:

- o receipt of a completed application which has been signed and notarized accompanied by proof of identity, which may include a copy of a driver's license, passport or other photo identification issued by a governmental entity.

- o other required verification will be obtained online, if possible, by board staff to include:

- o current licensure status.

- o national pharmacists' data bank.

- o national association of boards of pharmacy disciplinary database; and

- o nothing in this provision shall constitute a waiver of the requirements for licensure contained in 16.19.2 NMAC.

- License expiration. Pharmacist licenses under 16.19.2 NMAC shall expire six months after issue date.

16.19.31.10

PROVISIONS FOR PRACTITIONER CONTROLLED SUBSTANCES REGISTRATION DURING A DECLARED DISASTER:

- Emergency provisions for registration by endorsement. Practitioners currently possessing a temporary license issued by a New Mexico regulatory agency and possessing a current drug enforcement administration-controlled substance registration in a state in which a federal disaster has been declared may be registered by endorsement in New Mexico during the four months following the declared disaster at no cost with the following requirements:

- receipt of a completed application which has been signed and accompanied by proof of identity, which may include a copy of a driver's license, passport or other photo identification issued by a governmental entity.

- other required verification will be obtained online if possible, by board staff to include: current licensure status, national practitioners data banks; and

- nothing in this provision shall constitute a waiver of the requirements for licensure contained in 16.19.20 NMAC.

- Registration expiration. Practitioners' registrations issued under 16.19.20 NMAC shall expire six months after issue date.

16.19.31.11

PROVISIONS FOR PHARMACIST OR PHARMACY TECHNICIAN, UNAVAILABLE TESTING OR TRAINING:

- During a declared civil or public health emergency resulting in unavailable required testing or training, the board may authorize a temporary extension for a:

  - temporary pharmacist license under reciprocity issued pursuant to 16.19.3 NMAC.

  - pharmacy technician registration.

  - pharmacist to exercise prescriptive authority pursuant to 16.19.26 NMAC (e.g., current live basic life support/cardiopulmonary resuscitation).

- Pharmacists and technicians are to complete required testing or training as soon as practicable.

16.19.36.8

PHARMACIST IN CHARGE:

- All facilities compounding sterile preparations must designate a pharmacist in charge of operations who is licensed as a pharmacist in the state of residence of the facility.

- The pharmacist-in-charge is responsible for:
    - the development, implementation and continuing review and maintenance of written policies, procedures and SOP's which comply with USP/NF standards.
    - providing a pharmacist who is available for 24 hour seven-day-a-week services.
    - establishing a system to ensure that the CSP's prepared by compounding personnel are administered by licensed personnel or properly trained and instructed patients.
    - establishing a system to ensure that CSP's prepared by compounding personnel are prepared in compliance with USP/NF <797> (USP General Chapters: <797> Pharmaceutical Compounding-Sterile Preparations) standards.
    - ensuring facility personnel comply with written policies, procedures, and SOP's; and
    - developing an appropriate and individualized plan of care in collaboration with patient or caregiver and other healthcare providers for each patient receiving parenteral preparations in a home setting.

16.19.36.9

FACILITIES:

- The room or area in which compounded sterile preparations (CSP's) are prepared:

- must be physically designed and environmentally controlled to meet standards of compliance as required by USP/NF <797> (USP General Chapters: <797> Pharmaceutical Compounding-Sterile Preparations);

- must be periodically monitored, evaluated, tested, and certified by environmental sampling testing as required by USP/NF <797> (USP General Chapters: <797> Pharmaceutical Compounding-Sterile Preparations) with documentation retained for three years.

- must have a minimum of 100 square feet dedicated to compounding sterile preparations.

- the minimum size of a retail pharmacy must be 240 square feet; a retail pharmacy with preparation of sterile products capabilities must have 340 square feet with 100 square feet exclusive to compounding sterile preparations.

- the standalone CSP facility must have a minimum of 240 square feet with 100 square feet exclusive to compounding sterile preparations: and

- must be clean, lighted, and at an average of 80–150-foot candles; and

- must minimize particle generating activities.

- Addition of a compounding sterile preparations area in existing pharmacies will require submission of plans for remodeling to the board office for approval and inspection prior to licensure.

- A new CSP facility must comply with 16.19.6.8 NMAC through 16.19.6.11 NMAC of the regulations.

16.19.36.10

EQUIPMENT:

- Each facility compounding sterile preparations shall have sufficient equipment for the safe and appropriate storage, compounding, packaging, labeling, dispensing and preparation of compounded sterile preparations drugs and parenteral preparations appropriate to the scope of pharmaceutical services provided and as specified in USP/NF <797> (USP General Chapters: <797> Pharmaceutical Compounding-Sterile Preparations).

- All equipment shall be cleaned, maintained, monitored, calibrated, tested, and certified as appropriate to ensure proper function and operation with documentation retained for three years.

- Primary engineering controls used to provide an aseptic environment shall be tested in the course of normal operation by an independent qualified contractor and certified as meeting the requirements presented in USP/NF <797> (USP General Chapters: <797> Pharmaceutical Compounding-Sterile Preparations) at least every six months and when relocated, certification records will be maintained for three years.

- A library of current references (hard copy or electronic) shall be available including:
  - USP/NF or USP on Compounding: A Guide for the Compounding Practitioner.
  - New Mexico pharmacy laws, rules and regulations.
  - specialty references (stability and incompatibility references, sterilization and preservation references, pediatric dosing, and drug monograph references) as appropriate for the scope of services provided.

- Automated compounding devices shall:
  - have accuracy verified on a routine basis at least every 30 days per manufacturer's specifications.
  - be observed every 30 days by the operator during the mixing process to ensure the device is working properly.
  - have data entry verified by a pharmacist prior to compounding or have accurate final documentation of compounded preparations to allow for verification of ingredients by a pharmacist prior to dispensing; and
  - have accuracy of delivery of the end product verified according to written policies and procedures.

16.19.36.11

DOCUMENTATION REQUIRED:

- Written policies, procedures and SOPs consistent with USP/NF <797> (General Chapter <797> Pharmaceutical Compounding-Sterile Preparations) standards as well as those required below, must be established, implemented, followed by facility personnel, and available for inspection and review by authorized agents of the board of pharmacy.
- Written policies and procedures must be submitted to the state board of pharmacy prior to the issuance of any license. These records must include but are not limited to:
  - cleaning, disinfection, evaluation, validation, testing, certification, and maintenance of the sterile compounding area.
  - personnel qualifications, training, assessment and performance validation.

- o operation, maintenance, validation, testing, and certification of facility and equipment.
  - o SOP's for compounding, storing, handling, and dispensing of all components used and all compounded sterile preparations;
  - o SOP's for proper disposal of physical, chemical, and infectious waste.
  - o quality control guidelines and standards.
  - o quality assurance guidelines and standards.
  - o SOPs for determination of stability, incompatibilities, and drug interactions.
  - o error prevention and incident reporting policies and procedure as per 16.19.25 NMAC.
- All records required by this part shall be kept by the facility for at least three years and shall be readily available for inspection by the board or boards' agent.

16.19.36.12

RECORD KEEPING AND PATIENT PROFILE:

- The compounded sterile preparations facility is required to maintain patient's records which include but are not limited to the following.
- Prescription records or provider orders including the original prescription or original provider order, refill authorization, alterations in the original prescription or original provider order, and interruptions in therapy due to hospitalization.
- Patient's history including pertinent information regarding allergy or adverse drug reactions experienced by the patient.

- Patients receiving parenteral preparations in a home setting are contacted at a frequency appropriate to the complexity of the patient's health problems and drug therapy as documented on patient specific plan of care and with each new prescription, change in therapy or condition.

- Documentation that the patient receiving parenteral preparations in a home setting, or the agent has received a written copy of the plan of care and training in the safe administration of the medication.

16.19.36.13

REQUIREMENTS FOR TRAINING:

- All personnel, including pharmacists, pharmacists who supervise compounding personnel, pharmacists interns and pharmacy technicians , shall have completed didactic and experiential training with competency evaluation through demonstration and testing (written or practical) as required by USP/NF <797> (USP General Chapters: <797> Pharmaceutical Compounding-Sterile Preparations)and as outlined by the pharmacist-in-charge and described in the site policy and procedures or training manual, prior to compounding sterile preparations.

- Instructional topics shall include:
  - aseptic technique.
  - critical area contamination factors.
  - environmental monitoring.
  - facilities.
  - equipment and supplies.

- o sterile pharmaceutical calculations and terminology.

- o sterile pharmaceutical compounding documentation.

- o quality assurance procedures.

- o proper gowning and gloving technique.

- o the handling of cytotoxic and hazardous drugs; and

- o general conduct in the controlled area.

- o Training shall be obtained through completion of a site-specific, structured on-the-job didactic and experiential training program (not transferable to another practice site).

- Pharmacy technicians shall complete 100 hours of documented experiential training in compounded sterile preparations in accordance with Section 61-11-11.1 of the Pharmacy Act NMSA 1978 prior to compounding sterile preparations. Documentation of experiential training as defined in Subsection A of this section is transferrable to another practice site.

- Experiential training shall include those areas of training as outlined in USP <797> (USP General Chapters: <797> Pharmaceutical Compounding-Sterile Preparations) with appropriate observational assessment and testing of performance as outlined in USP <797> (USP General Chapters: <797> Pharmaceutical Compounding-Sterile Preparations) including glove fingertip and media fill tests.

- All personnel, including pharmacists compounding sterile hazardous drugs, pharmacists supervising compounding personnel, pharmacy interns compounding sterile hazardous drugs, and pharmacy technicians compounding sterile hazardous drugs, shall have completed didactic and experiential training with competency evaluation through demonstration and written or practical testing as required by USP/NF in addition to training in sterile non-hazardous preparations as listed above. Training will be conducted as outlined by the pharmacist-in-charge and described in the site policy and procedures or training manual and shall be completed prior to compounding sterile hazardous preparations.

- Frequency of training and assessment shall be conducted as required by USP <797> (USP General Chapters: <797> Pharmaceutical Compounding-Sterile Preparations) to assure continuing competency and include:
  - o initial training before compounding sterile preparations.
  - o annual refresher training and assessment in didactic topics.
  - o annual testing of glove fingertip and media fill for low and medium risk compounding.
  - o six-month testing of glove fingertip and media fill testing for high-risk compounding.

- Documentation of training: Written documentation of initial and in-service training, the results of written or practical testing, and process validation of compounding, personnel shall be retained for three years and contain the following information:
  - o name of person receiving the training or completing the testing or process validation.
  - o date(s) of the training, testing, or process validation.
  - o general description of the topics covered in the training or testing or of the process validated.
  - o name of person supervising the training, testing, or process validation.
  - o signature of the person receiving the training or completing the testing or process validation and the pharmacist-in-charge or other pharmacist employed by the pharmacy and designated by the pharmacist-in-charge as responsible for training, testing, or process validation of personnel.

16.19.36.14

PATIENT OR CAREGIVER TRAINING FOR USE OF COMPOUNDED STERILE PREPARATIONS IN A HOME SETTING:

- The pharmacist shall maintain documentation that the patient has received training consistent with Subsection F of 16.19.4.16 NMAC.

- The facility shall provide a 24-hour toll free telephone number for use by patients of the pharmacy.

- There shall be a documented, ongoing quality assurance program that monitors patient care and pharmaceutical care outcomes, including the following:
  - routine performance of prospective drug use review and patient monitoring functions by a pharmacist.
  - patient monitoring plans that include written outcome measures and systems for routine patient assessment.
  - documentation of patient training.

16.19.36.15

QUALITY ASSURANCE OF COMPOUNDED STERILE PREPARATIONS:

- There shall be a documented, ongoing performance improvement control program that monitors personnel performance, equipment, and facilities:
  - all aspects of sterile product preparation, storage, and distribution, including details such as the choice of cleaning materials and disinfectants and monitoring of equipment accuracy shall be addressed in policy and procedures.

- if non-sterile to sterile bulk compounding of more than 25 units of compounded sterile preparations is performed using non-sterile chemicals, containers, or devices, and the results of appropriate end product testing must be documented prior to the release of the product from quarantine; the test must include appropriate tests for particulate matter and pyrogens.

- there shall be documentation of quality assurance audits at regular, planned intervals, including infection control and sterile technique audits; a plan for corrective action of problems identified by quality assurance audits shall be developed which includes procedures for documentation of identified problems and action taken; a periodic evaluation as stated in the policy and procedures of the effectiveness of the quality assurance activities shall be completed and documented.

- the batch label of each sterile compounded product shall contain:

- drug product name(s), diluent names(s), and amount(s) of each.

- batch lot or control number.

- final concentration(s), and volume when appropriate, solution ingredient names and amounts.

- beyond use date, and time when applicable.

- route of administration when applicable.

- date of preparation.

- facility identifier: name or initials of person preparing the product and, if prepared by supportive personnel, the name or identifying initials and the name or initials of the pharmacist that completed the final check.

- when appropriate, ancillary instructions such as storage instructions or cautionary systems, including hazardous material warning labels and containment bags; and

- o device instructions when needed.

- o the patient specific label of a CSP shall contain:

- o patient name.

- o solution, ingredient names, amounts.

- o beyond use date, and time when applicable.

- o route of administration;

- o directions for use, including infusion rates, specific times scheduled, when appropriate and applicable.

- o identifier of person preparing the product and, if prepared by supportive personnel (i.e., pharmacist intern or pharmacy technician), the identifier of the pharmacist that completed the final check.

- o when appropriate, ancillary instructions such as storage instructions or cautionary systems, including hazardous material warning labels and containment bags; and

- o device instructions when needed.

- o if dispensed for other than inpatient use, the label shall include all other required information.

- There shall be a mechanism for tracking and retrieving products which have been recalled. If batch preparation of compounded sterile preparations is being performed, a record must be maintained for each batch.

- A formulation record shall provide a consistent source document (recipe) for CSP preparation and shall include the following:

  - o name, strength, dosage form, and final volume of the compounded preparation.

  - o all ingredients and their quantities.

  - o equipment needed to prepare the CSP, when appropriate, and mixing instructions.

- other environmental controls, such as the duration of mixing and other factors pertinent to consistent preparation of the CSP.

- beyond use dating, the container for dispensing, storage requirements, and quality control procedures; and

- information needs for proper labeling (e.g. sample label).

- The compounding record for each CSP batch shall verify accurate compounding in accordance with the formulation record and shall include:

  - reference to the formulation record for the CSP.

  - name, strength, volume, manufacturer, and manufacturer's lot number for each component.

  - name, strength, and volume of the finished CSP.

  - reconciliation of actual yield with anticipated yield, and total number of CSP units produced.

  - identifier of person preparing the product and, if prepared by support personnel (i.e., pharmacist intern or pharmacy technician), the identifier of the pharmacist that completed the final check;

  - date of preparation.

  - batch lot or control number assigned.

  - assigned beyond use date, and time when appropriate.

  - results of applicable quality control procedures.

16.19.37.8

LICENSURE OR REGISTRATION:

- Any outsourcing facility that is engaged in the compounding of sterile drugs in this state shall be registered as an outsourcing facility under the Federal Food, Drug, and Cosmetic Act and be licensed as an outsourcing facility in this state.

- Any nonresident outsourcing facility, that distributes or causes to be distributed, compounded sterile drugs into New Mexico shall be registered as an outsourcing facility under the Federal Food, Drug, and Cosmetic Act and be licensed as a nonresident outsourcing facility.

- No outsourcing facility shall ship, mail or deliver controlled substances in or into this state unless registered by the Drug Enforcement Administration (DEA) and the board for controlled substances.

- Applications for a nonresident outsourcing facility under this section shall be made on a form furnished by the board. The board may require such information as it deems is reasonably necessary to carry out the purposes of this section.

- The board shall not issue an initial or renewed license for an outsourcing facility unless the facility furnishes the board with a report, issued by the appropriate regulatory agency of the resident state, or entity approved by the appropriate regulatory agency of the resident state, or by the FDA, of an inspection that has occurred within the 12 months immediately preceding receipt of the license application by the board (with no intervening change in outsourcing facility ownership). The board may deny licensure unless the applicant submits

- documentation satisfactory to the board that any deficiencies noted in an inspection report have been corrected.

- No license shall be issued or renewed for an outsourcing facility unless the applicant supplies the board with proof of such registration by the FDA.

- No license shall be issued or renewed for a non-resident outsourcing facility that is required to be licensed or registered by the state in which it is physically located unless the applicant supplies the board with proof of such licensure or registration. The board may establish, by rule, standards for the licensure of an outsourcing facility that is not required to be licensed or registered by the state in which it is physically located.

- The license fee shall be as specified in 16.19.12 NMAC and shall be renewed biennially before the last day of December each year.

- The board may deny, revoke, or suspend an outsourcing facility's registration for any violation of the state drug laws.

16.19.37.9

OPERATIONAL STANDARDS:

- The following minimum standards shall apply to all outsourcing facilities and dual-purpose facilities for which licenses have been issued by the board:

- All drugs and chemicals used in the manufacturing process or held for sale shall conform to the Drug, Device and Cosmetic Act and shall be stored, preserved and disposed of as prescribed by laws regulating the labeling and manufacture of drugs. When necessary, and/or according to label requirements, all drugs and chemicals which require refrigeration shall be stored and preserved under proper temperature.

- Facilities must comply with applicable FDA current good manufacturing practice requirements as set forth in title 21, CFR, Subsection 211.1 to 211.208 inclusive (or successor regulations). The definitions and interpretations contained in Section 201 of the Federal Food and Drug Act shall be applicable.

- Facilities must be in compliance with applicable DEA regulations.

- Facilities must comply with applicable United States Pharmacopeia requirements.

16.19.37.10

MINIMUM REQUIREMENTS:

PHARMACIST IN CHARGE.

- Any drugs compounded in an outsourcing facility or dual-purpose facility licensed pursuant to this rule shall be compounded by or under the direct supervision of a licensed pharmacist and in accordance with all applicable federal and state laws.

- Any drugs repackaged in an outsourcing facility licensed pursuant to this rule shall be repackaged by or under the direct supervision of a licensed pharmacist and in accordance with all applicable federal and state laws.

- The pharmacist in charge shall be responsible for the maintenance and implementation of appropriate policies and procedures.

- The pharmacist in charge shall be responsible for ensuring proper training and competence of personnel for all duties assigned to or undertaken by personnel.

- The pharmacist in charge shall be responsible for ensuring personnel are properly licensed or registered with the board.

- The pharmacist in charge shall be responsible for compliance with all federal regulations applicable to outsourcing facilities, and all regulations administered by the board.

DUAL PURPOSE FACILITY.

- No outsourcing facility may dispense any drug to any person pursuant to a prescription unless it is also licensed as a pharmacy (or nonresident pharmacy) in this state and meets all other applicable requirements of federal and state law.

- Required records of the outsourcing facility shall be maintained separate from required records of the pharmacy.

RESTRICTIONS.

- Any drugs compounded in an outsourcing facility licensed pursuant to this rule shall be compounded in accordance with all applicable federal and state laws.

- Any drugs repackaged in an outsourcing facility licensed pursuant to this rule shall be repackaged in accordance with all applicable federal and state laws.

- Each repackaged drug product is also accompanied by a copy of the prescribing information that accompanied the original drug product that was repackaged.

- The drug product is included on a report submitted to FDA each June and December identifying the drug products made by the outsourcing facility during the previous six month period, and providing the active ingredient(s); source of the active ingredient(s); national drug code (NDC) number of the source ingredient(s), if available; strength of the active ingredient(s) per unit; the dosage form and route of administration; the package description; the number of individual units produced; and the NDC number of the final product, if assigned.

LABELING OF DRUGS COMPOUNDED OR REPACKAGED BY AN OUTSOURCING FACILITY.

- The label of any drug compounded by an outsourcing facility shall include, but not be limited to the following:
    - a statement that the drug is a compounded drug or a reasonable comparable alternative statement that prominently identifies the drug as a compounded drug.
    - the name, address, and phone number of the applicable outsourcing facility; and
    - with respect to the drug:
    - the lot or batch number.
    - the established name of the drug.
    - the dosage form and strength.
    - the statement of quantity or volume, as appropriate.
    - the date that the drug was compounded.
    - the expiration date.
    - storage and handling instructions.
    - the NDC number, if available.
    - the statement that the drug is not for resale, and if the drug product is distributed by an outsourcing facility other than pursuant to a prescription for an individual identified patient, the statement "office use only";
    - a list of the active and inactive ingredients, identified by established name, and the quantity or proportion of each ingredient.
- The label on the immediate container (primary packaging, e.g., the syringe) of the repackaged product includes the following:

133

- the statement "this drug product was repackaged by (name of outsourcing facility)";

- the address and phone number of the outsourcing facility that repackaged the drug product.

- the established name of the original, approved drug product that was repackage.

- the lot or batch number of the repackaged drug product.

- the dosage form and strength of the repackaged drug product.

- a statement of either the quantity or volume of the repackaged drug product, whichever is appropriate.

- the date the drug product was repackaged.

- the beyond use date of the repackaged drug product.

- storage and handling instructions for the repackaged drug product.

- the NDC number of the repackaged drug product, if available.

- the statement "not for resale," and, if the drug product is distributed by an outsourcing facility other than pursuant to a prescription for an individual identified patient, the statement "office use only";

- when included on the label of the FDA approved drug product from which the drug product is being repackaged, a list of the active and inactive ingredients, unless such information is included on the label for the container from which the individual units are removed, as described below:

- the label on the container from which the individual units are removed for administration (secondary packaging, e.g., the bag, box, or other package in which the repackaged products are distributed) includes.

- the active and inactive ingredients, if the immediate drug product label is too small to include this information.

- the directions for use, including, as appropriate, dosage and administration, and the following information to facilitate adverse event reporting: www.fda.gov/medwatch and 1-800-FDA-1088.

CONTAINER.

- The container from which the individual units of the drug are removed for dispensing or for administration (such as a plastic bag containing individual product syringes) shall include:
    - a list of active and inactive ingredients, identified by established name, and the quantity or proportion of each ingredient; and
    - any other information required by regulations promulgated by the commissioner to facilitate adverse event reporting in accordance with the requirements established in Section 310.305 of title 21 of the Code of Federal Regulations (CFR).

BULK DRUGS.

- A drug may only be compounded in an outsourcing facility that does not compound using bulk drug substances as defined in Section 207.3(a)(4) of title 21 of the CFR or any successor regulation unless:
    - the bulk drug substance appears on a list established by the FDA identifying bulk drug substances for which there is a clinical need.
    - the drug is compounded from a bulk drug substance that appears on the federal drug shortage list in effect at the time of compounding, distributing, and dispensing.
    - if an applicable monograph exists under the USP-NF, or another compendium or pharmacopeia recognized by the FDA and the bulk drug substances each comply with the monograph; and

o   the bulk drug substances are each manufactured by an establishment that is registered with the federal government.

INGREDIENTS.

- When an outsourcing facility uses ingredients, other than bulk drug substances, such ingredients must comply with the standards of the applicable USP-NF monograph, if such monograph exists, or of another compendium or pharmacopeia recognized by the FDA for purposes of this subdivision, if any.

UNSAFE OR INEFFECTIVE DRUGS.

- No outsourcing facility may compound or repackage a drug that appears on a list published by the FDA that has been withdrawn or removed from the market because such drugs or components of such drugs have been found to be unsafe or not effective.

PROHIBITION ON WHOLESALING.

- No compounded or repackaged drug will be sold or transferred by any entity other than the outsourcing facility that compounded or repackaged such drug. This does not prohibit the administration of a drug in a health care setting or dispensing a drug pursuant to a properly executed prescription.

PROHIBITION AGAINST COPYING AN APPROVED DRUG.

- No outsourcing facility may compound a drug that is essentially a copy of one or more approved drugs.

PROHIBITION AGAINST COMPOUNDING DRUGS PRESENTING DEMONSTRABLE DIFFICULTIES.

- No outsourcing facility may compound a drug:

- that is identified, directly or as part of a category of drugs, on a list published by the FDA that present demonstrable difficulties for compounding that are reasonably likely to lead to an adverse effect on the safety or effectiveness of the drug or category of drugs, taking into account the risks and benefits to patients; or

- that is compounded in accordance with all applicable conditions identified on the drug list as conditions that are necessary to prevent the drug or category of drugs from presenting demonstrable difficulties.

DISPENSING, COMPOUNDING, AND SALE OF DRUGS; LIMITATIONS.

- A resident pharmacy shall limit the interstate dispensing of compounded sterile human drug preparation to five percent of the total prescriptions dispensed by that pharmacy, unless registered with the FDA and the board as an outsourcing facility. This requirement will be effective at the time it becomes enforced by the FDA in states that have not entered into a memorandum of understanding with the FDA.

ADVERSE EVENT REPORTS.

- Outsourcing facilities shall submit a copy of all adverse event reports submitted to the FDA in accordance with the content and format requirements established in section 310.305 of title 21 of the CFR, or any successor regulation, to the executive director of the board. Upon request, follow up reports required by the FDA shall be submitted to the executive director of the board.

- Outsourcing facilities shall develop and implement written processes for the surveillance, receipt, evaluation, and reporting of adverse events for the drug products it compounds or repackages as described in 310.305(a) and 211.198 of title 21 of the CFR.

DRUG THAT IS THE SUBJECT OF A REMS.

- If the outsourcing facility compounds from a drug that is the subject of a REMS approved with elements to assure safe use, or from a bulk drug substance that is a component of such drug, the outsourcing facility must demonstrate to FDA before beginning to compound that it will use controls comparable to the controls applicable under the REMS.

DRUG RECORDS.

- Outsourcing facilities shall establish and maintain inventories and records of all transactions regarding the receipt and distribution or other disposition of compounded sterile drugs. These records shall include the following information:
  - the identity and quantity of the drugs received and distributed or disposed of.
  - the dates of receipt and distribution or other disposition of the drugs.
  - the name, location and license number of the business, health care practitioner or other entity appropriately licensed to possess, dispense, distribute, administer, or destroy prescription drugs.
- There shall be a mechanism for tracking and retrieving products that have been recalled.
- Resident outsourcing facilities shall maintain compounded sterile preparation batch records in accordance with Subsection B of 16.19.36.15 NMAC.
- A record of drugs repackaged must be kept, and include the following: the name and strength of the drug, lot number, name of manufacturer or distributor, beyond use date, date of repackaging, total number of dosage units repackaged, quantity or volume per repackaged container, number of dosage units wasted, initials of repackager and of pharmacist performing final check.

- All drugs repackaged by a pharmacist intern or pharmacy technician must undergo a final check by the pharmacist.

- Every registrant under the Controlled Substances Act, manufacturing, distributing or dispensing a controlled substance shall maintain, on a current basis, a complete and accurate record of each substance manufactured, received, sold or delivered by him in accordance with regulations of the board.

- Records shall be kept by all persons licensed pursuant to the Pharmacy Act of all dangerous drugs, their receipt, withdrawal from stock and use or other disposal. The records shall be open to inspection by the board or its agents, and the licensee shall be responsible for the maintenance of the records in proper form.

- Records required by board-administered law or regulation shall be available for inspection and photocopying by the board's state drug inspectors for three years.

PART-TWO

NEW MEXICO PHARMACY LAW QUESTIONS

1. The pharmacist is required to complete _____30 hours of continuing education every two years for renewing his/her license.

    a.   10 days

    b.   15 days

    c.   30 days

    d.   45 days

2. A minimum of _____ hours per renewal period shall be in the subject area of pharmacy law offered by the New Mexico board of pharmacy.

    a.   1 hour

    b.   2 hours

    c.   3 hours

    d.   4 hours

3. According to New Mexico State Pharmacy Law, the prescription record should be kept on file for:

    a.   Two years from the date of dispensing.

    b.   Five years from the date of dispensing.

    c.   Three years from the date of dispensing.

    d.   A year from the date of dispensing.

4. In New Mexico, pharmacy permits expire on which of the following dates each year?

    a.   November 30

    b.   January 31

    c.   October 30

    d.   December 31

5. An emergency oral prescription for Schedule II controlled drugs must be mailed to dispensing pharmacy by an authorized prescriber within:

    a.   48 hours after an oral authorization.

    b. 7 days after an oral authorization.

    c. 10 days after an oral authorization.

    d. 72 hours after an oral authorization.

6. According to New Mexico State Pharmacy Law, a remote tele-pharmacy is limited to filling no more than _____ prescriptions per day.

    a. 50

    b. 100

    c. 200

    d. 450

7. According to New Mexico State Pharmacy Law, a new telephone prescription for any Schedule III, IV, or V opiate shall not exceed:

    a. 3-day supply

    b. 5-day supply

    c. 10-day supply

    d. None of the above

8. How often shall the data related to sale, distribution or dispensing of Schedule V pseudoephedrine products be submitted to the Board?

    a. Every 15 days

    b. Every 5 days

    c. Every 48-hour

    d. Every 7 days

9. In New Mexico, how many times can a prescription for Nalbuphine (Nubain) be refilled?

    a. Cannot be refilled

    b. 5 times

    c. As Needed within 1-year

    d. Maximum 10 times

10. The pharmacist-in-charge shall report to the Board on the Board approved forms for any dispensing error within:

    a. 72-hour of the discovery.

    b. 7 days of the discovery.

    c. 10 days of the discovery.

    d. 15 days of the discovery.

11. The pharmacy shall maintain a record of prescriptions which are returned to stock. The record shall include patient name, date filled, prescription number, drug name, drug strength, and drug quantity. The record shall be retrievable within:

    a. 24 hours

    b. 48 hours

    c. 72 hours

    d. Immediately

12. The prescription area of a retail pharmacy in New Mexico WITHOUT the preparation of sterile products capabilities must be minimum of:

    a. 50 square feet

    b. 150 square feet

    c. 240 square feet

    d. 500 square feet

13. In Mexico, how long do interns have to notify the board of changes in address?

    a. Within 5 days

    b. Within 10 days

    c. 5Within 15 days

    d. Within 20 days

14. In Mexico, how many days prior to the initiation of an automated drug distribution system must the PIC provide the board with a written notice?

    a. 10 days prior

    b. 15 days prior

    c. 300 days prior

    d. 60 days prior

15. In Mexico, how long does a pharmacist have to review the withdrawal record of medication from a nurse in a hospital where the pharmacy was closed?

    a. 24 hours

    b. 36 hours

    c. 48 hours

    d. 72 hours

16. In Mexico, how many days does a paper script have to stay on the licensed premises from the initial date of dispensing?

    a. 60 days

    b. 90 days

    c. 120 days

    d. 150 days

17. In Mexico, what is the minimum prescription area in square feet?

    a. 120 square feet

    b. 180 square feet

    c. 240 square feet

    d. 320 square feet

18. A pharmacist receives a prescription for 40 Percocet tablets, but the pharmacy has only 15 tablets in stock. The patient accepts the 15 tablets. How much time does the pharmacist have to provide the remaining 25 tablets?

    a. 24 hours

    b. 72 hours

    c. 96 hours

    d. 6 months

19. Which of the following is a correct DEA number for a Dr. Andrea J. Shedlock, who was Dr. Andrea Costello when she requested her DEA number before she was married?

    a. AC1234563

    b. AS1234563

    c. JC1234563

    d. JS1234563

20. What form is used to report the theft of con- trolled substances?

    a. DEA Form 41

    b. DEA Form 106

    c. DEA Form 222

    d. DEA Form 224

21. What classification of drug recall will cause serious adverse health consequences or death?

    a. Class I

    b. Class II

    c. Class III

    d. Class IV

22. Which of the following addresses nonsterile compounding?

    a. ISO 9000

    b. USP 790.

    c. USP 795.

    d. USP 797.

23. What is the maximum amount of pseudoephedrine base that may be purchased in 1 day?

    a. 2.4 g

    b. 3.6 g

    c. 9 g

    d. 10 g

24. How long is a pharmacy's DEA permit valid?

    a. 1 year

    b. 2 years

    c. 3 years

    d. 4 years

25. What is DEA form 222 used for?

    a. To report the theft of controlled substances.

    b. To document the destruction of controlled substances.

    c. To order Schedule II medications.

    d. To prescribe Schedule II medications.

26. The Red Book is a resource that focuses on:

    a. Therapeutic equivalence evaluations.

    b. Labeled and unlabeled uses of medications.

    c. Pharmacokinetics.

    d. Drug pricing.

27. If a drug has no accepted medical use and extremely high potential for abuse, which DEA schedule would it be categorized in?

    a. Schedule I.

    b. Schedule II.

    c. Schedule III.

    d. Schedule IV.

28. Schedule II medication must be stored in:

    a. A refrigerator.

    b. A locked safe.

    c. A laminar hood.

    d. The DEA cabinet.

29. How much time does a physician have to provide a written prescription for an "emergency prescription"

    for a Schedule II drug?

    a. 24 hours

    b. 48 hours

    c. 72 hours

    d. 7 days

30. How long is a prescription valid if it has "prn" refills written on it by the physician?

    a. 1 month

    b. 6 months

    c. 1 year from the date the prescription was written

    d. As many as needed

31. What is the maximum number of refills allowed on a prescription of lorazepam if authorized by a

    physician?

    a. None

    b. Five

    c. 12

    d. Unlimited

32. How many refills are allowed on C-IV drugs?

    a. 5

    b. 3

    c. 1

    d. 0

33. Which of the following potential hazards are addressed by OSHA regulations?

    a. Exposure to wet surfaces and potential slip and falls.

    b. Exposure to bloodborne pathogens.

    c. Exposure to hazardous chemicals.

    d. All of these potential hazards are addressed by OSHA regulations.

34. What is medication therapy management?

    a. Proper storage and handling of medication

    b. Medication-related advertising that is directed to consumers from drug manufacturers

    c. Medication-related information provided to physicians and other health care professionals by pharmacists

    d. A service or group of services that optimize therapeutic outcomes for individual patients

35. A pharmacist receives a prescription for 40 Percocet tablets, but the pharmacy has only 15 tablets in stock. The patient accepts the 15 tablets. How much time does the pharmacist have to provide the remaining 25 tablets?

    a. 24 hours

    b. 72 hours

    c. 96 hours

    d. 6 months

36. Prescription Monitoring Programs focus is:

    I.   Administration of controlled substance

    II.   Dispensing of controlled substance

    III.   Transportation of controlled substance

    IV.   Prescribing of controlled substance

    a.   I and II only

    b.   II and III only

    c.   III and IV only

    d.   II and IV only

37. Which of the following is needed to be labeled on the unit-dose-package?

    I.   The drug's name

    II.   The drug's strength

    III.   The expiration dates

    IV.   Lot number

    a.   I and II only

    b.   II and III only

    c.   III and IV only

    d.   I, II, III, and IV only

38. Emergency refills are allowed when:

   I.   Failure to fill the prescription might result in an interruption of therapy.

   II.   Pharmacist is unable to reach the prescriber after reasonable effort.

   III. Pharmacist is unable to reach the prescriber due to natural disaster.

   IV.   Failure to fill the prescription might create patient suffering.

       a. I and II only

       b. II and III only

       c. III and IV only

       d. I, II, III, and IV

39. Per Federal laws, how long does the pharmacy keep records of schedule II drugs?

       a. 2 years

       b. 3 years

       c. 5 years

       d. 7 years

40. The information related to transfer of a prescription maintained by each pharmacy shall at least include:

   I.   Dispensing date of the prescription.

   II.   Number of refills remaining.

   III. Original date of the prescription.

   IV.   Number of refills authorized.

a. I and II only

b. II and III only

c. III and IV only

d. I, II, III, and IV

41. According to federal laws, what is the minimum time between an initial and third purchase of Schedule V OTC drug?

    a. 24 hours

    b. 48 hours

    c. 72 hours

    d. 120 hours

42. What are the total days of supply of Simvastatin 20 mg prescription that may be dispensed with authorized refills, as long as it doesn't exceed the total quantity authorized by the prescriber?

    a. 30 days

    b. 60 day

    c. 90 days

    d. 120 days

43. Per Federal law what is the quantity limit of schedule II drugs to be dispensed at a time?

    a. 30 days

    b. 60 days

    c. 90 days

    d. 120 days

44. A prescription is written for metformin 500 mg tablets BID. How long this prescription should be kept on file?

   a. 6 months

   b. 1 year

   c. 2 years

   d. 3 years

45. How many refills are allowed for Xanax?

   a. 3 refills in 6 months

   b. 4 refills in 6 months

   c. 5 refills in 6 months

   d. 6 refills in 5 months

46. If the drug is labeled August 2020, what date does the drug expire?

   a. 08/01/2020

   b. 08/31/2020

   c. 07/01/2020

   d. 07/31/2020

47. What is the maximum day supply of the medication the pharmacy can dispense for an emergency situation like natural disaster fill?

    a.   10 days

    b.   14 days

    c.   30 days

    d.   60 days

48. Per Federal law if a prescription fails to send a cover prescription for the controlled drug, the pharmacy shall notify the Bureau of Narcotic Enforcement in writing within:

    a.   80 hours of the prescriber's failure to do so.

    b.   120 hours of the prescriber's failure to do so.

    c.   144 hours of the prescriber's failure to do so.

    d.   160 hours of the prescriber's failure to do so.

49. Medicaid/Medicare records of patient's are required to be stored for at least:

    a.   5 years

    b.   7 years

    c.   10 years.

    d.   12 years.

50. A prescriber may authorize a maximum of how many refills on a prescription for Percodan tablets?

    a.   0

    b.   1

    c.   2

d. 5

e. 10

51. Which of the following drugs or devices does not require a patient package Insert (PPI)?

   I.   Conjugated estrogens.

   II.   Progesterone containing drugs.

   III. Intrauterine devices.

   IV.   Oral contraceptives.

   a. II only

   b. I and II only

   c. I, II, III only

   d. I, II, III and IV

52. A prescription for a controlled substance II must include the following information EXCEPT:

   a. Patient's name

   b. Patient's address

   c. DEA registration number

   d. Number of refills

53. Which of the following schedule II prescription elements CANNOT be changed with the prescriber's permission?

   a. Drug quantity

   b. Dosage form

   c. Direction of use

   d. Drug name

54. An exact count is allowed for schedule IV product in a container that holds greater or equal to

_____ capsules or tablets.

   a. 500

   b. 1000

   c. 1500

   d. 2000

55. The prescriber shall keep records of the information on the prescription label for:

   a. 2 years

   b. 3 years

   c. 4 years

   d. 5 years

56. According to Federal law, what is the drug classification for Mazindol?

   a. Schedule II

   b. Schedule III

   c. Schedule IV

   d. Schedule V

57. DEA form 222 must exclusively contain only these substances EXCEPT:

   a. Carfentanil

   b. Etorphine HCL

   c. Diprenorphine

   d. Hydromorphone

58. Per Federal law which of the following may be sold without a prescription?

    a.   Pregabalin

    b.   Tramadol

    c.   Modafinil

    d.   Robitussin AC

59. A practitioner may dispense directly to ultimate user a controlled substance classified in Schedule II in an amount not to exceed:

    a.   48-hours supply

    b.   72-hours supply

    c.   120-hours supply

    d.   180-hours supply

60. All prescription records for non-controlled substances shall be maintained on the licensed premises for a period of _____ from the date of dispensing.

    a.   1 year

    b.   2 years

    c.   3 years

    d.   4 years

61. What must be found on all controlled substance prescriptions?

    a.   Pharmacy DEA number

    b.   Physician's business license number

    c.   Physician's DEA number

    d.   Physician's license number

62. A prescription for **Xanax** is valid for:

    a.   4 months

    b.   5 months

    c.   6 months

    d.   12 months

63. Which of the following is an example of 3 file storage system?

    a.   Schedule I, Schedule II- III, Schedule V

    b.   Schedule II, Schedule III-V, Non-scheduled

    c.   Schedule I, Schedule II- V, Non-scheduled

    d.   Schedule II, Schedule III, Schedule IV, Schedule V

64. If a prescription is written for a 90-day supply, then what is the expiration term for this prescription?

    a.   Original plus 2 refills

    b.   Original plus 3 refills

    c.   Original plus 4 refills

    d.   Original plus 11 refills

65. When a pharmacist partially fills controlled substance II, the remaining portion of a schedule II prescription may be filled within:

    a. 24-hours of the first partial filling.

    b. 36-hours of the first partial filling.

    c. 48-hours of the first partial filling.

    d. 72-hours of the first partial filling.

66. What is the schedule for 100 mg of dihydrocodeine in a 100 ml solution (including non-narcotic ingredients)?

    a. Schedule II

    b. Schedule III

    c. Schedule IV

    d. Schedule V

67. Which of the following medications requires an exact count as an inventory?

    a. Soma

    b. Vimpat

    c. Halcion

    d. Percocet

68. A prescription of allopurinol 100 mg, # 180 prescribed for "office use" by Dr. Bilal: What course of action would you take?

    a. Fill the entire prescription

    b. Only fill 30 tablets

    c. Fill after verifying the prescription

    d. Don't fill. Prescription for office use is not acceptable.

69. If a pharmacy partially fills a schedule II prescription, upon each partial fill the pharmacist must document:

   I.   Date of fill.

   II.   The quantity dispensed.

   III. The remaining quantity.

   IV.   The pharmacist's sign.

   a. I and II only

   b. II and III only

   c. III and IV only

   d. I, II, III, and IV

70. Patient counseling is required for:

   I.   New prescription pick-up

   II.   Each medication refills

   III. Medicaid patient's prescription

   IV.   Older than 50 years age

   a. I and II only

   b. II and III only

   c. III and IV only

   d. I and III only

71. Which form is used to report lost or stolen drugs?

   a. DEA 41

   b. DEA 222

   c. DEA 224

   d. DEA 106

72. Prescription labeling requirement is exempted for:

   I.   Mail order pharmacy

   II.   Internet pharmacy

   III.   Inpatient hospital pharmacy

   IV.   Outpatient community pharmacy

   a. I and II only

   b. II and III only

   c. III only

   d. I, II, III, and IV

73. Which of the following is TRUE about schedule II prescription?

   I.   It can be refilled.

   II.   It can be transferred.

   III.   It can be faxed.

   IV.   It can be emailed.

   a. II only

   b. III only

   c. IV only

   d. None of the above.

74. The partial filling of a schedule II drugs for terminally ill patients must be carried out within:

    a.   10 days from the initial filling

    b.   96 hours from the initial filling.

    c.   30 days from the initial filling.

    d.   72 hours from the initial filling

75. The prescriber is mandated to return the hardcopy prescription within _____ days after giving over the phone schedule II emergency supply per Federal law.

    a.   24 hours

    b.   72 hours

    c.   7 days

    d.   10 days

PART-TWO

NEW MEXICO PHARMACY LAW QUESTIONS

1. Answer: C

    The pharmacist is required to complete 30 hours of continuing education every two years for renewing his/her license.

    (1). A minimum of 1.0 CEU (10 contact hours) excluding the law requirement, per renewal period shall be obtained through "live programs" that are approved as such by the ACPE or the accreditation council for continuing medical education (ACCME). Live programs provided by other providers (such as continuing nursing education) may be acceptable based on review and approval of the board.

2. Answer: B

    A minimum of 0.2 CEU (2 contact hours) per renewal period shall be in the subject area of pharmacy law offered by the New Mexico board of pharmacy.

    (4). The board of pharmacy will accept CPE education units for programs or activities completed outside the state; provided, the provider has been approved by the ACPE (NOT CME-II) under its' criteria for quality at the time the program was offered.

3. Answer: C

    According to New Mexico State Pharmacy Law, the original paper prescription document must be maintained for a minimum of three years and the electronic image of the prescription for ten years.

4. Answer: D

    In New Mexico, a pharmacy permit expires on December 31 of each year.

5. Answer: B

7 days after an oral authorization. An emergency oral prescription for Schedule II controlled drugs must be written to reduce and mailed to dispensing pharmacy by an authorized prescriber within 7 days after an oral authorization, [New Mexico Administrative Code (NMAC) 16.19.20.47(B)(3)].

Emergency dispensing of Schedule II controlled substances. "Emergency situation" means the prescribing physician determines:

(1). that immediate administration of a controlled substance is necessary for proper treatment of the intended patient;

(2). that no appropriate alternative treatment is available, including administration of a drug which is not a controlled substance under Schedule II; and

(3). that it is not reasonably possible for the prescribing practitioner to provide a written prescription to be presented to the person dispensing the substance prior to the dispensing.

B. A pharmacy may dispense a Schedule II controlled substance in the above instance only if he receives oral authorization of a practitioner or authorization via facsimile machine and provided:

(1). the quantity prescribed is limited to the amount needed to treat the patient during the emergency period;

(2). the pharmacist shall reduce the prescription to a written form, and it contains all information required of a Schedule II controlled substance prescription except the signature of the prescribing practitioner:

(3). the prescribing physician, within 7 days after authorization of the emergency dispensing, shall furnish a written, signed prescription to the pharmacist.

The signed prescription shall have written on the face "AUTHORIZATION FOR EMERGENCY DISPENSING" and the date of the oral order or facsimile order;

(4). the signed prescription shall be attached to the oral emergency prescription order or the facsimile emergency prescription order and be filed as other Schedule II prescriptions.

6. Answer: C

200 prescriptions, [New Mexico Administrative Code (NMAC) 16.19.33.9(16)].

A remote tele-pharmacy is limited to filling no more than 200 prescriptions per day. If filling more than 200 prescriptions per day, the remote tele-pharmacy shall be converted to a retail pharmacy and is subject to all applicable requirements of 16.19.6 NMAC.

7. Answer: C

10 day supply, [New Mexico Administrative Code (NMAC) 16.19.20.42 (F)].

A pharmacist may dispense directly a controlled substance listed in Schedule III or IV, which is a prescription drug as determined under the New Mexico Drugs and Cosmetics Act, only pursuant to either a written prescription signed by a practitioner or a facsimile of a written, signed prescription transmitted by the practitioner or the practitioner's agent to the pharmacy or pursuant to an oral prescription made by an individual practitioner and promptly reduced to written form by the pharmacist containing all information required for a prescription except the signature of the practitioner.

8. Answer: D

Every 7 days, [New Mexico Administrative Code (NMAC) 16.19.20.53(B)(5)].

Pharmacies shall submit the information collected to the board or its agents. Pharmacies will submit data every seven (7) days beginning September 15, 2013. Pharmacies may petition the executive director of the board for an alternative method for the submission of the information collected pursuant to this section.

9. Answer: B

5 times within a period of 6-months, [New Mexico Administrative Code (NMAC) 16.19.20.68(E)(4)].

Under New Mexico State Pharmacy Law, Nalbuphine (Nubain) is classified as a Schedule IV controlled drug and can be refilled 5 times within a period of 6 months.

10. Answer: D

15 days of the discovery, [New Mexico Administrative Code (NMAC) 16.19.25.8].

The pharmacist-in-charge shall:

A. Develop and implement written error prevention procedures as part of the Policy and Procedures Manual.

B. Report incidents, including relevant status updates, to the Board-on-Board approved forms within fifteen (15) days of the discovery.

11. Answer: C

72 hours, [New Mexico Administrative Code (NMAC) 16.19.6.14(B)].

The pharmacy shall maintain a record of prescriptions which are returned to stock. The record shall include patient name, date filled, prescription number, drug name, drug strength, and drug quantity.

The record shall be retrievable within 72 hours.

12. Answer: C

240 square feet, [New Mexico Administrative Code (NMAC) 16.19.6.10(A),(C) and (D) and 16.19.36.9].

The restricted area to be occupied by the prescription department shall be an undivided area of not less than 240 square feet. The floor area shall extend the full length of the prescription compounding counter.

This area shall provide for the compounding and dispensing and storage of all dangerous or restricted drugs, pharmaceuticals, or chemicals under proper condition of sanitation, temperature, light, ventilation, segregation and security.

No space in this area shall provide for an office, auxiliary store room or public restroom(s).

The prescription compounding counter must provide a minimum of 16 square feet of unobstructed compounding and dispensing space for one pharmacist and a minimum of 24 square feet for two or more pharmacists when on duty concurrently.

The counter shall be of adequate height of at least 36 inches, if necessary, five-percent or at least one work station will comply with the American with Disabilities Act. D. The restricted floor area shall be unobstructed for a minimum width of 30 inches from the prescription compounding center.

The room or area in which compounded sterile preparations (CSP's) are prepared:

a. must be physically designed and environmentally controlled to meet standards of compliance as required by USP/NF 797.

b. must have a minimum of 100 square feet dedicated to compounding sterile preparations;

c. the minimum size of a retail pharmacy must be 240 square feet; a retail pharmacy with preparation of sterile products capabilities must have 340 square feet with 100 square feet exclusive to compounding sterile preparations;

d. the stand-alone CSP facility must have a minimum of 240 square feet with 100 square feet exclusive to compounding sterile preparations;

e. must be clean, lighted, and at an average of 80-150 foot candles; and

f. must minimize particle generating activities.

13. Answer: B

In Mexico, interns have to notify the board of changes in address within 10 days.

14. Answer: D

In Mexico, the initiation of an automated drug distribution system must be provided by PIC to the board with a written notice 60 days prior.

15. Answer: D

In Mexico, a pharmacist has to review the withdrawal record of medication from a nurse in a hospital where the pharmacy was closed within 72 hours.

16. Answer: C

In Mexico, a paper script has to stay on the licensed premises from the initial date of dispensing within 120 days.

17. Answer: C

In Mexico, the minimum prescription area in 240 square feet.

18. Answer: B

The Controlled Substances Act allows for the partial filling of a Schedule II medication prescription, with the remaining medication to be provided to the patient within 72 hours or the quantity becomes void.

19. Answer: A

The first letter of a physician's DEA number will be A, B, F, or M. The second letter is the first letter of the physician's last name at the time he or she applied for the DEA number. DEA numbers are required as a result of the Controlled Substances Act.

20. Answer: B

On discovery of a theft of controlled sub- stances, the local law enforcement agency must be notified, and DEA Form 106 needs to be submitted.

21. Answer: A

A class I drug recall may cause irreversible injury or possibly death to a patient, a class II drug recall may cause reversible harm to the patient, and a class III drug recall does not cause injury to the patient.

22. Answer: C

USP, 795. Addresses no sterile compounding, and USP, 797. Deals with sterile compounding.

23. Answer: B

Under the Combat Methamphetamine Epidemic Act of 2005, the maximum amount of pseudoephedrine that may purchase in a single day is 3.6 g; the maximum amount that may be purchased in a 30-day time period is 9 g.

24. Answer: C

The Controlled Substances Act specifies that a DEA permit is valid for 3 years.

25. Answer: C

Form 222 is a triplicate order form for schedule 1 and 2 controlled substances. The purchaser submits copy 1 and 2 to the supplier and keeps copy 3 on file.

26. Answer: D

The Red Book is the leading resource for information on drug pricing.

27. Answer: A

Schedule I includes drugs such as Marijuana, Ecstasy, Peyote, and Heroin.

28. Answer: B

All schedule II substances should be stored in a locked safe, while schedule III, IV and V may be stored throughout the pharmacy.

29. Answer: D

According to the Controlled Substances Act, a physician has up to 7 calendar days to provide a pharmacy a handwritten prescription for a Sched- ule II medication if it was called in to the pharmacy. The quantity prescribed should be enough to last only until the patient can see the physician.

30. Answer: C

Although the expression "prn" means as needed, a prescription with "prn" refills can only be refilled up to 1 year from the date the medication was prescribed.

Any additional refills require the prescriber's approval.

31. Answer: B

Lorazepam is classified as a Schedule IV medication under the Controlled Substance Act and is permitted to be refilled a maximum of five times within 6 months of the prescription's being written.

32. Answer: A

CIII drugs can have up to 5 refills and are refillable up to 6 months. Some examples of C-IV drugs include Xanax.

33. Answer: D

OSHA regulations address the following potential hazards in a pharmacy: Exposure to bloodborne pathogens (HIV, Hepatitis B & C), exposure to hazardous chemicals or drugs, exposure of eyes or bodies to corrosive materials, exposure to latex allergy, exposure to wet surfaces that could cause slip and falls, and availability of personal protective equipment.

34. Answer: D

Medication storage and handling, as well as both consumer and professional information, may be parts of medication therapy management, but the more comprehensive definition of a service or group of services that optimize therapeutic outcomes for individual patients is the best answer.

35. Answer: B

The Controlled Substances Act allows for the partial filling of a Schedule II medication prescription, with the remaining medication to be provided to the patient within 72 hours or the quantity becomes void.

36. Answer: D

Prescription Monitoring Programs focus is dispensing and prescribing of controlled substance.

37. Answer: D

Unit-dose-package label include:

- The drug's name

- The drug's strength

- The expiration dates

- Lot number

38. Answer: D

   All the above conditions may qualify to refill emergency prescription.

39. Answer: A

   Per Federal laws, the pharmacy keeps records of schedule II drugs for 2 years

40. Answer: D

   The information related to transfer of a prescription maintained by each pharmacy shall at least include:

   - Dispensing date of the prescription.

   - Number of refills remaining.

   - Original date of the prescription.

   - Number of refills authorized.

41. Answer: B

   According to federal laws, it is 48 hours.

42. Answer: C

   A pharmacy may dispense accelerated refills of up to a 90-day supply of medication pursuant to a valid prescription that may be dispensed with authorized refills, as long as it doesn't exceed the total quantity authorized by the prescriber.

43. Answer: C

   There is 90-day supply limit to all schedule II drugs per federal laws.

44. Answer: B

Metformin is a legend drug, and the prescription should be kept on file for 2 years.

45. Answer: C

Xanax is classified as controlled substances (schedule IV).

46. Answer: B

The drug expires the last day of the month.

47. Answer: C

The maximum day supply of the medication the pharmacy can dispense for an emergency situation like natural disaster fill is 30 days' supply.

48. Answer: C

If a prescription fails to send a cover prescription for the controlled drug, the pharmacy shall notify the Bureau of Narcotic Enforcement in writing within 144 hours of the prescriber's failure to do so.

49. Answer is C

Records related to Medicaid/Medicare patients are required to be stored for at least.

10 ears.

50. Answer: A

Schedule II drugs has no refills.

51. Answer: D

All the above drugs or devices does not require a patient package Insert (PPI).

52. Answer: D

C-II prescriptions don't have refills.

53. Answer: D

Following elements of schedule II prescription cannot be changed/added:

- Patient's name

- Drug name

- Prescriber's name

- Prescriber's signature

54. Answer: B

   An exact count is allowed for schedule III- V products in a container that holds greater or equal to 1000 capsules or tablets.

55. Answer: B

   The prescriber shall keep records of the information on the prescription label for 3 years.

56. Answer: C

   Mazindol – Schedule IV drug per Federal law

57. Answer: D

   Hydromorphone can be mentioned on DEA form 222 with other drugs. But not carfentanil, etorphine HCL, and diprenorphine.

58. Answer: D

   Per Federal law Robitussin AC may be sold without a prescription.

59. Answer: B

   A practitioner may dispense directly to un ultimate user a controlled substance classified in Schedule II in an amount not to exceed 72-hours supply.

60. Answer: A

   All prescription records for non-controlled substances shall be maintained on the licensed premises for a period of one year from the date of dispensing.

61. Answer: C

The Controlled Substances Act requires that all prescribers and dispensers of controlled sub-stances have a DEA number. The requirement shows the pharmacist that the physician has the authority to prescribe controlled substances.

62. Answer: C

A prescription for schedule III to IV is valid for 6 months.

63. Answer: B

3 file storage system means: Schedule II, Schedule III-V, Non-scheduled.

64. Answer: B

90 days = 1 months plus 3 refills

65. Answer: D

When a pharmacist partially fills controlled substance II, the remaining portion of a schedule II prescription may be filled within 72-hours of the first partial filling.

66. Answer: D

100 mg/100 ml of dihydrocodeine solution is a schedule V drug.

67. Answer: D

Schedule II drug Percocet requires an exact count for inventory.

68. Answer: D

The prescription should not be filled because a prescription is the incorrect method to order drugs "for office use."

69. Answer: D

The pharmacist must document upon each partial fill:

- Date of fill.

- The quantity dispensed.

- The remaining quantity.

- The pharmacist's sign.

70. Answer: D

   Patient counseling is required for new prescription pick-up and Medicaid patient's prescription.

71. Answer: D

   Stolen medications reported via DEA form 106.

72. Answer: C

   Prescription labeling requirement is exempted for inpatient hospital pharmacy.

73. Answer: D

   It cannot be refilled, transferred or faxed it can be faxed only on few exceptions.

74. Answer: B

   An opioid treatment program certification shall be granted for a term not to exceed 3 years.

75. Answer: C

   The prescriber is mandated to return the hardcopy prescription within SEVEN days after giving over the phone schedule II emergency supply.

REFERENCES

1. DEA's Diversion Control Division Website www.DEAdiversion.usdoj.gov

2. DEA Homepage www.dea.gov

3. U.S. Government Publishing Office

4. https://www.govinfo.gov Provides access to the CFR, Parts 1300 to End, primary source for the Pharmacist's Manual, and the Federal Register which contains proposed and finalized amendments to the CFR.

5. Office of National Drug Control Policy (ONDCP) www.whitehouse.gov/ondcp

6. Food and Drug Administration www.FDA.gov

7. SAMHSA www.samhsa.gov

8. CSAT https://www.samhsa.gov/about-us/who-we-are/offices-centers/csat

9. Federation of State Medical Boards www.FSMB.org

10. National Association of Boards of Pharmacy https://nabp.pharmacy

11. National Association of State Controlled Substances Authorities www.nascsa.org

Made in the USA
Coppell, TX
20 October 2024